HUMAN ANATOMY
COLORING BOOK FOR KIDS

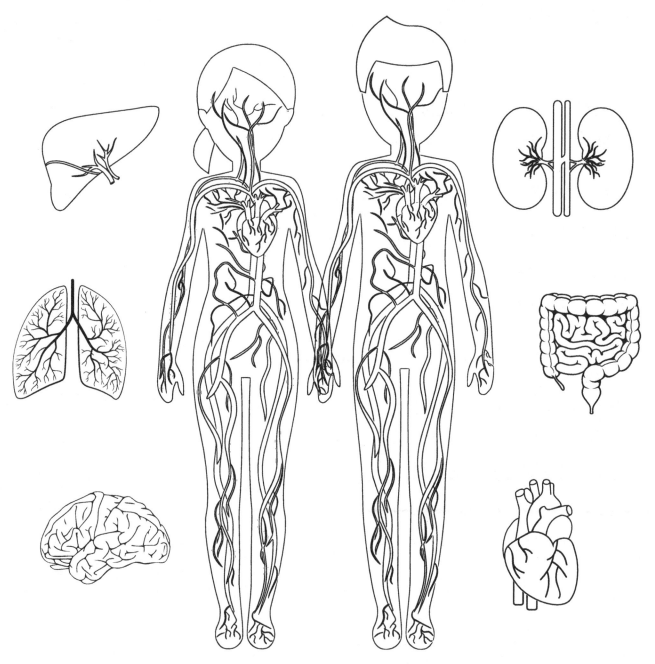

© All rights reserved to Anatomy by Heart

TABLE OF CONTENTS

I. SKELETAL SYSTEM .... (5-17)
- SKULL ANATOMY 7
- SPINE ANATOMY 9
- HUMAN RIBS 11
- HUMAN HAND STRUCTURE 13
- HUMAN FOOT STRUCTURE 15
- BONE STRUCTURE 17

II. MUSCULAR SYSTEM .... (19-25)
- UPPER BODY MUSCLES 19
- LOWER BODY MUSCLES 21
- ARM ANATOMY 23-25

III. BRAIN ANATOMY 27

IV. EYE ANATOMY 29

V. EAR ANATOMY 31

VI. MOUTH ANATOMY .... (33-39)
- HUMAN TEETH 35
- TOOTH STRUCTURE 37
- HUMAN TONGUE 39

VII. DIGESTIVE SYSTEM .... (41-43)

VIII. RESPIRATORY SYSTEM .... (45-47)
- GAS EXCHANGE 47

TABLE OF CONTENTS

IX. MALE REPRODUCTIVE SYSTEM... 49

X. FEMALE REPRODUCTIVE SYSTEM 51

XI. FEMALE BREAST ANATOMY 53

XII. HEART ANATOMY .... (55-57)

- HEART BLOOD FLOW 57

XIII. SKIN ANATOMY 59

XIV. VAGUS NERVE 61

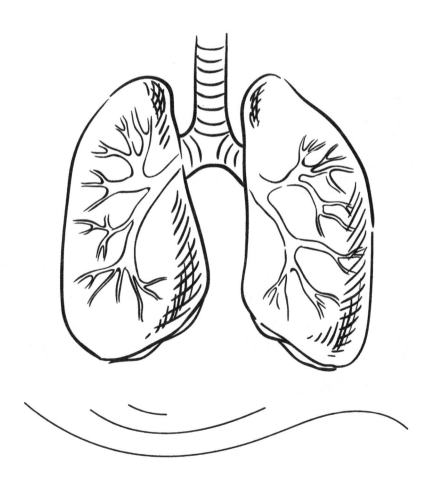

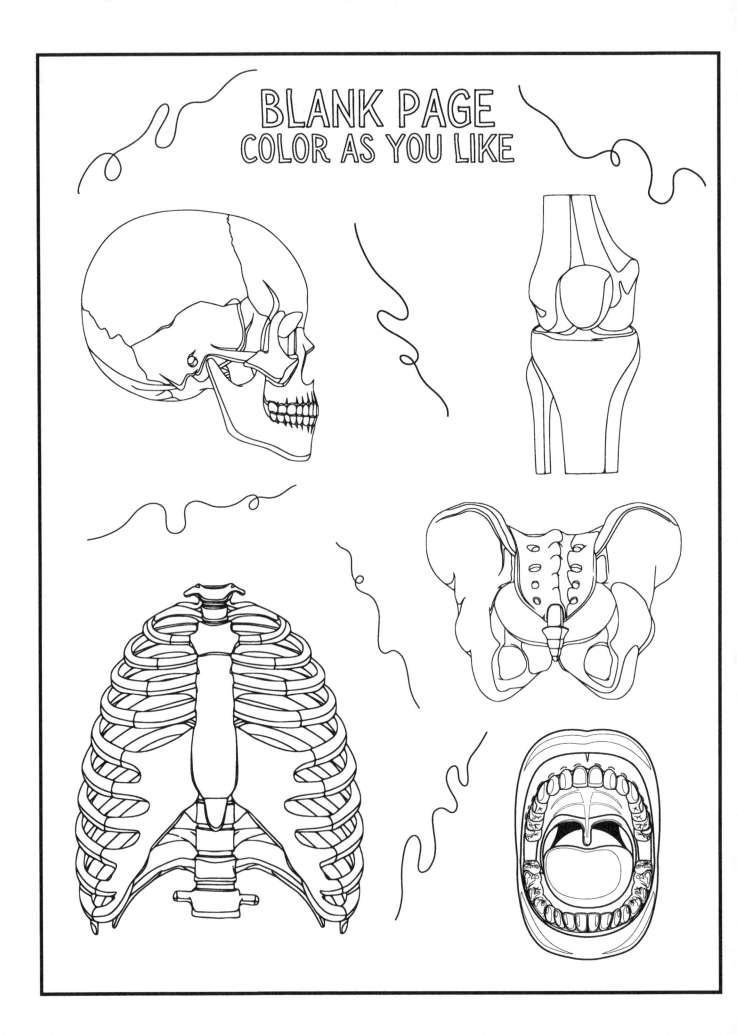

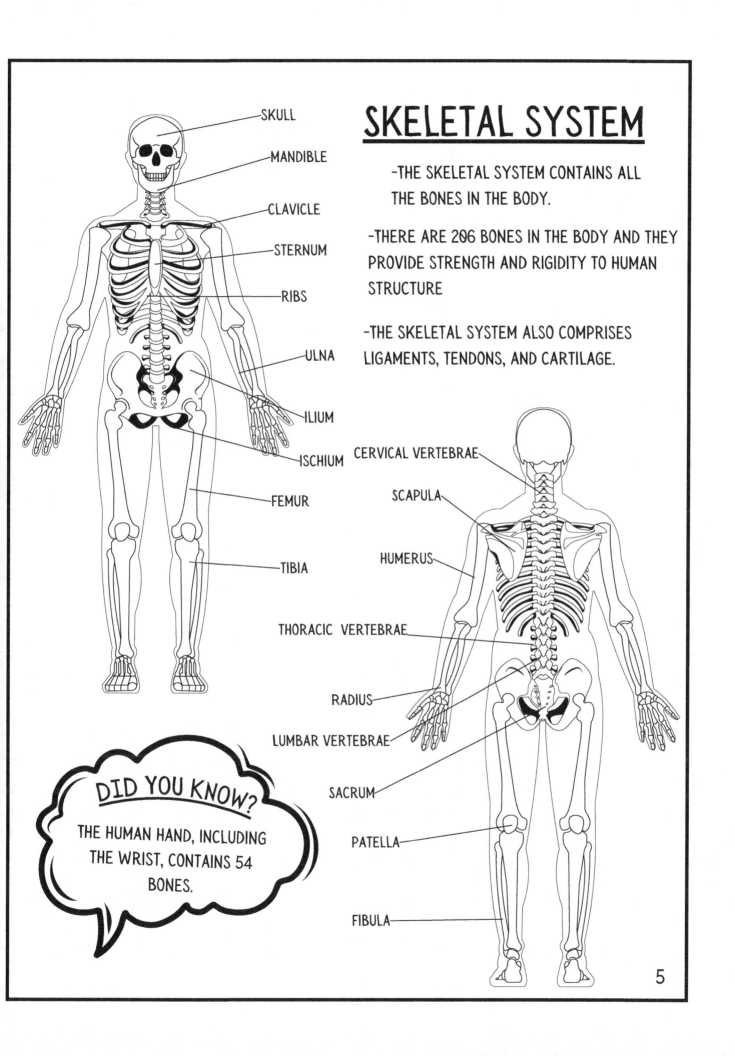

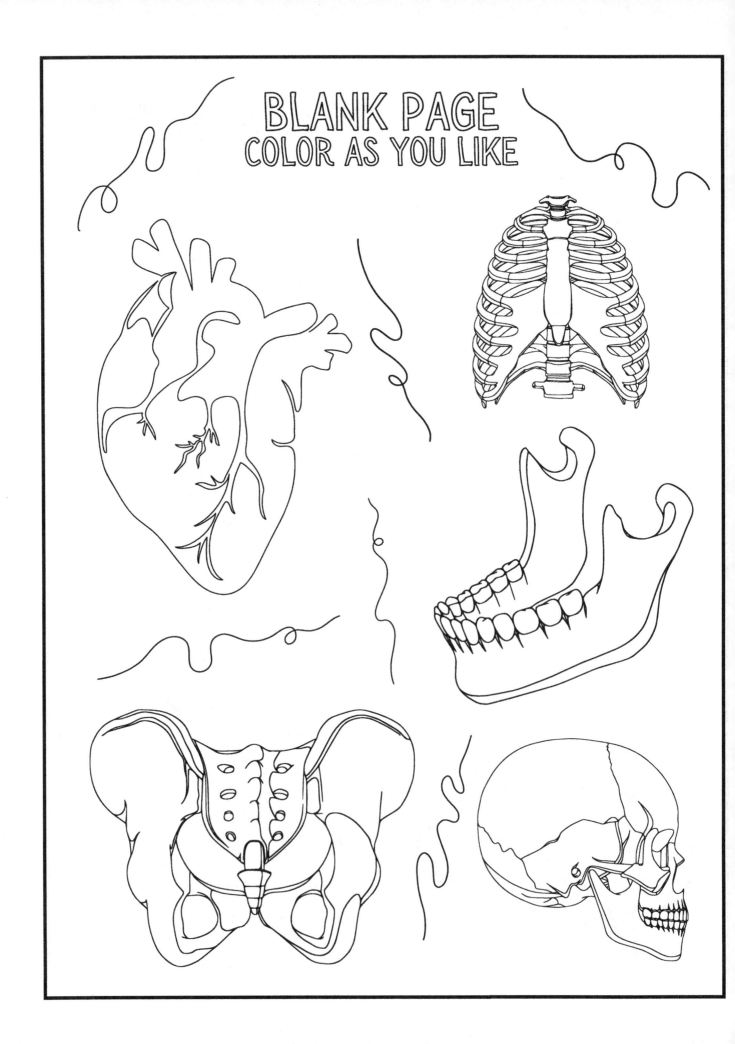

SKULL ANATOMY

- THE SKULL IS A BONY STRUCTURE THAT PROTECTS THE BRAIN AND GIVES SUPPORT TO THE FACE

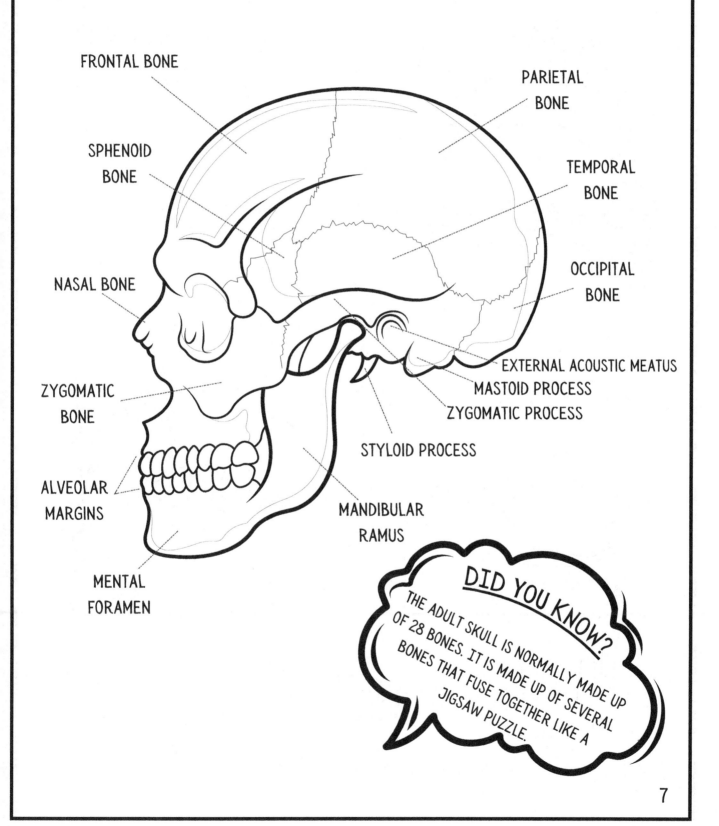

DID YOU KNOW?
THE ADULT SKULL IS NORMALLY MADE UP OF 28 BONES. IT IS MADE UP OF SEVERAL BONES THAT FUSE TOGETHER LIKE A JIGSAW PUZZLE.

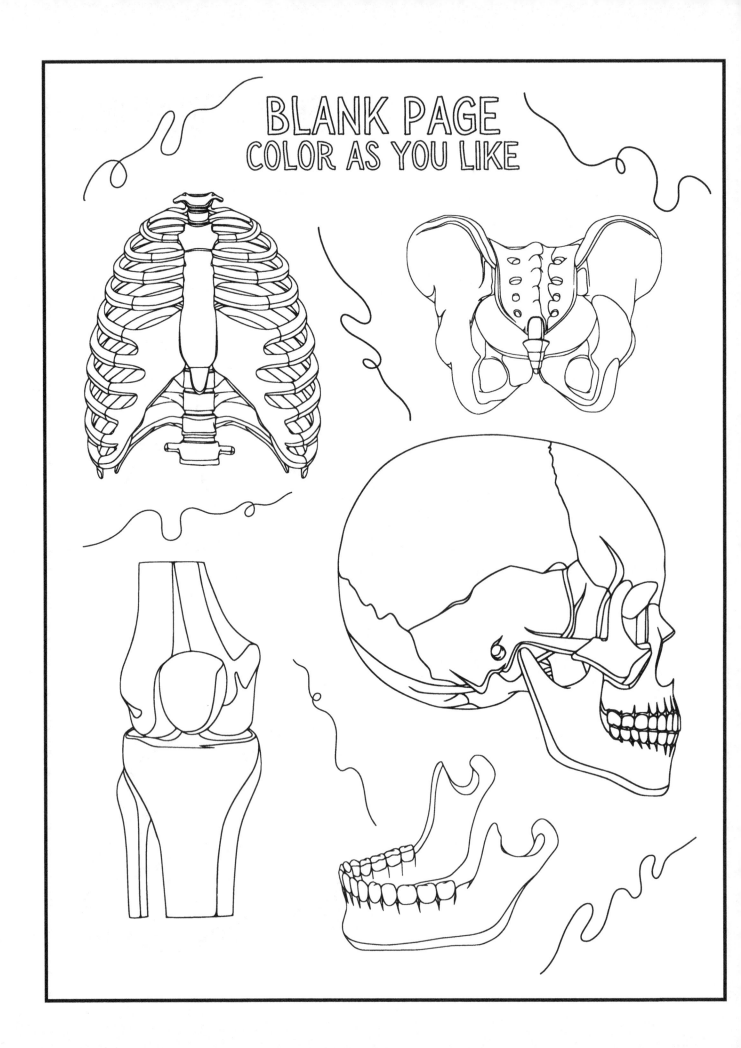

SPINE ANATOMY

-SPINE IS RESPONSIBLE FOR YOUR BODY STRUCTURE AND SUPPORT YOU TO MOVE FREELY AND TO BEND WITH FLEXIBILITY.

CERVICAL

-CERVICAL SPINE PROVIDES SUPPORT FOR YOUR HEAD, AND ALLOWS FOR A WIDE RANGE OF HEAD MOTIONS.

THORACIC

-THORACIC SPINE HELPS STABILIZE YOUR RIB CAGE. TOGETHER, THEY PROTECT YOUR HEART AND LUNGS.

-THORACIC MOBILITY IS ESSENTIAL FOR CORRECT EXPANSION OF THE RIBCAGE WHILE WE BREATHE.

LUMBAR

-LUMBAR SPINE SUPPORTS YOUR BODY'S WEIGHT AND IT'S THE CENTER OF YOUR BODY'S BALANCE

SACRUM

COCCYX

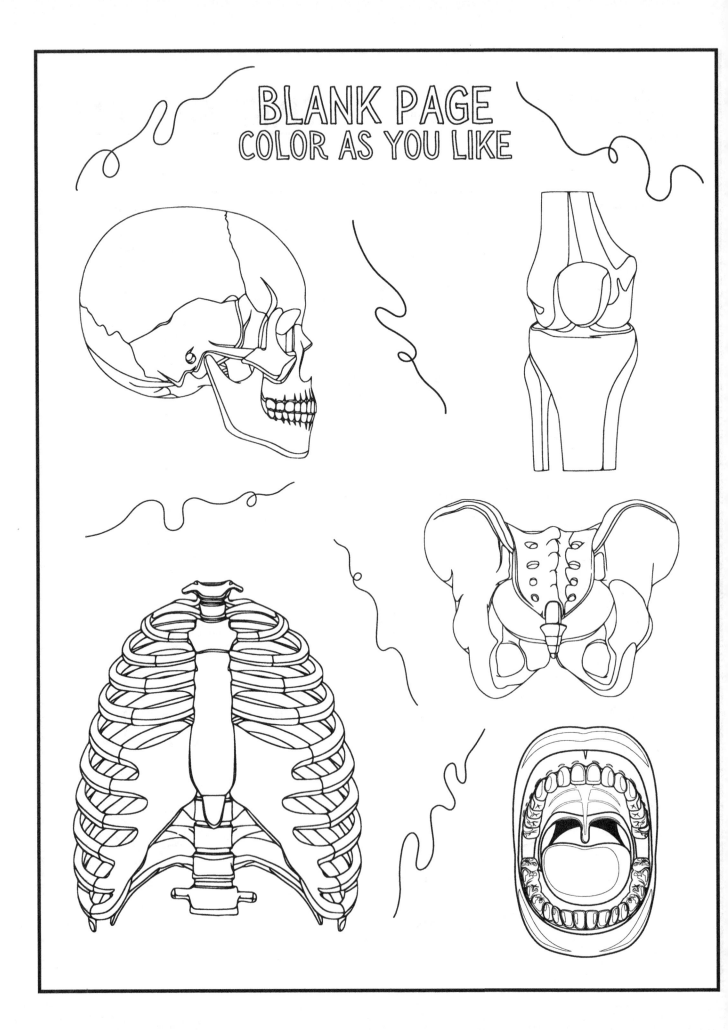

HUMAN RIBS

- THERE ARE 12 PAIRS OF RIB BONES WITH ONE ON EACH SIDE OF THE CHEST

- THE RIB CAGE IS FOUND IN THE CHEST REGION AND IT PROTECTS YOUR INTERNAL ORGANS FROM DAMAGE.

DID YOU KNOW?
THE BONES ARE FILLED WITH BONE MARROW

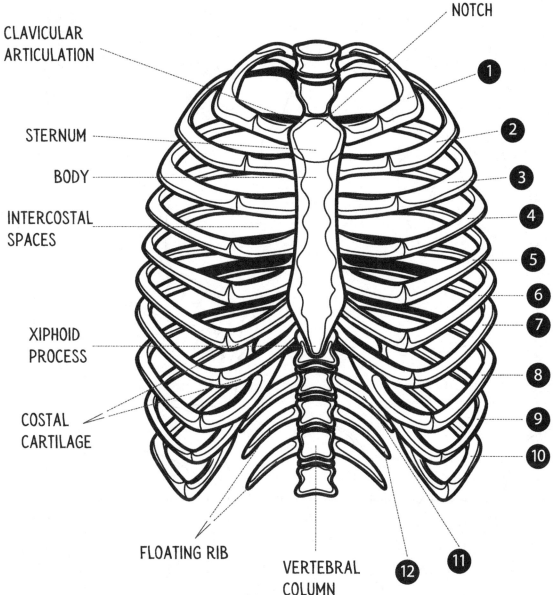

Labels: CLAVICULAR ARTICULATION, STERNUM, BODY, INTERCOSTAL SPACES, XIPHOID PROCESS, COSTAL CARTILAGE, FLOATING RIB, VERTEBRAL COLUMN, JUGULAR NOTCH, 1-12

- THE RIBS THAT JOIN TO THE STERNUM ARE CALLED TRUE RIBS WHILE THE RIBS THAT JOIN INDIRECTLY THROUGH THE CARTILAGE ARE CALLED FALSE RIBS. THE RIBS (11&12) ARE CALLED FLOATING RIBS BECAUSE THEY DO NOT ATTACH TO THE STERNUM AT ALL.

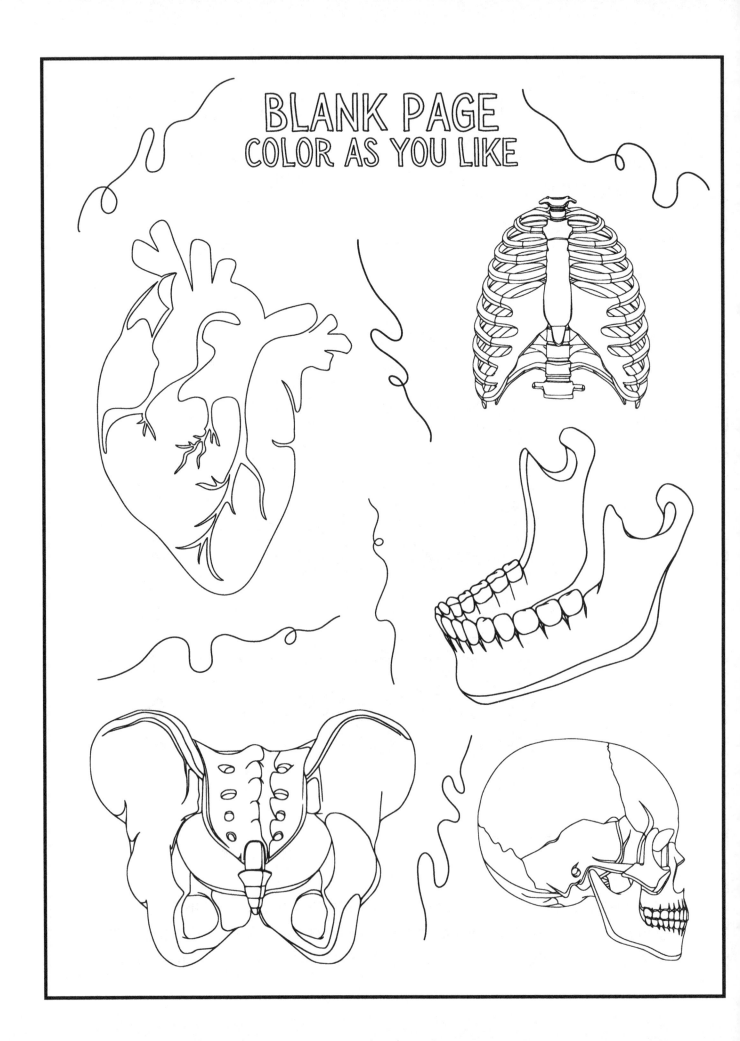

HUMAN HAND STRUCTURE

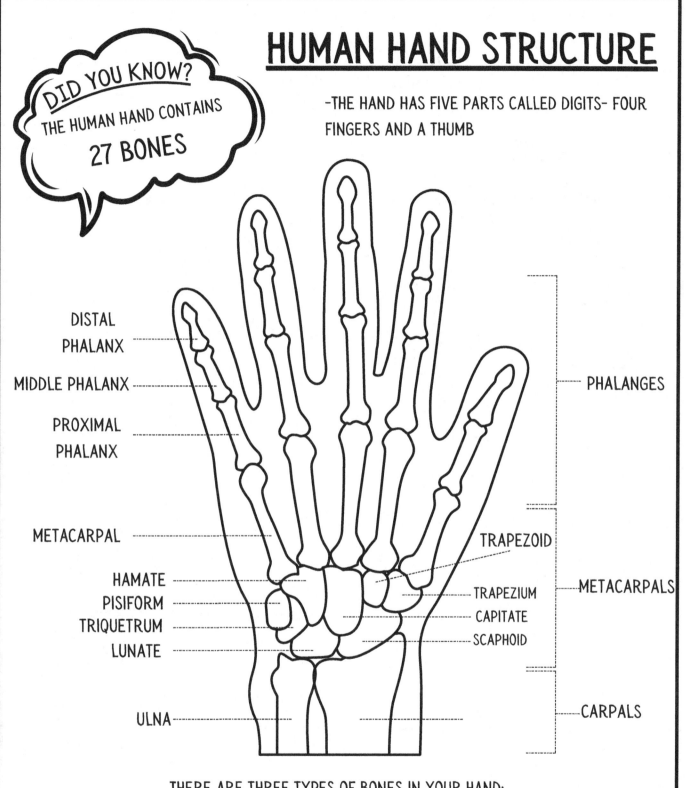

DID YOU KNOW? THE HUMAN HAND CONTAINS **27 BONES**

- THE HAND HAS FIVE PARTS CALLED DIGITS- FOUR FINGERS AND A THUMB

Labels: DISTAL PHALANX, MIDDLE PHALANX, PROXIMAL PHALANX, METACARPAL, HAMATE, PISIFORM, TRIQUETRUM, LUNATE, ULNA, TRAPEZOID, TRAPEZIUM, CAPITATE, SCAPHOID, PHALANGES, METACARPALS, CARPALS

THERE ARE THREE TYPES OF BONES IN YOUR HAND:
- PHALANGES IN THE FINGERS (14 IN NUMBER)
- METACARPALS IN THE MID-HAND (5 IN NUMBER)
- CARPALS IN THE WRIST (8 IN NUMBER).

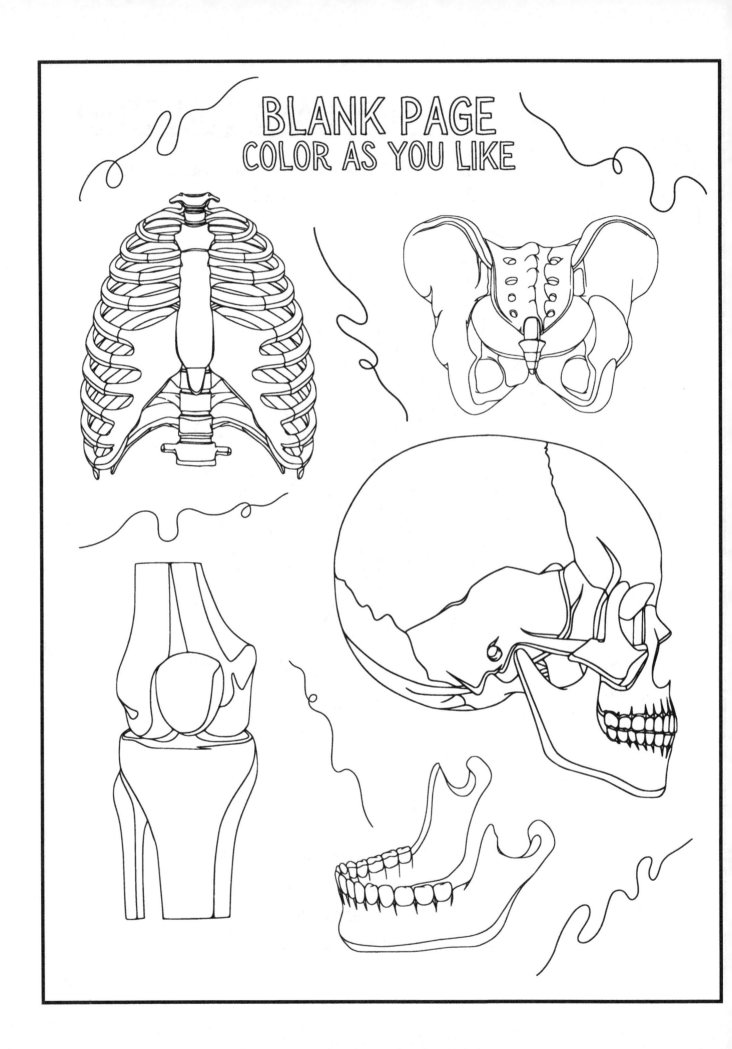

HUMAN FOOT STRUCTURE

-ONE HUMAN FOOT HAS 33 JOINTS AND 26 BONES. THAT'S ALMOST ONE-QUARTER OF ALL THE BONES IN YOUR BODY.

-THE MAIN FUNCTION OF TIBULA AND TIBIA IS TO PROVIDE SATBILITY TO THE ANKLE JOIN

DID YOU KNOW? THERE ARE ARE 8,000 NERVES IN YOUR FEET

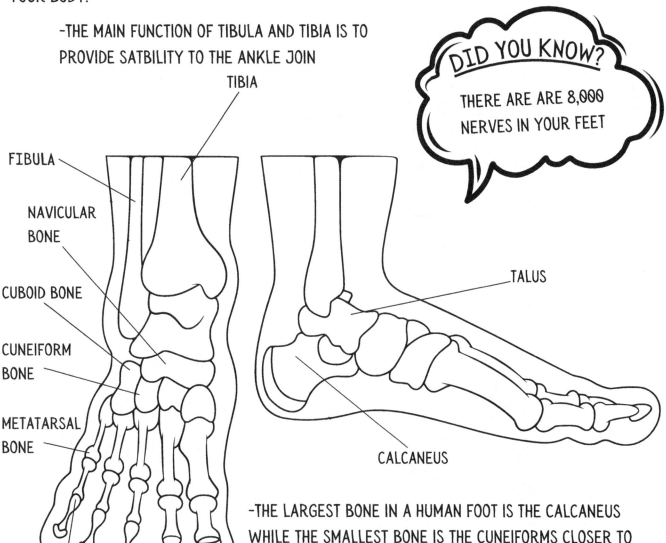

- TIBIA
- FIBULA
- NAVICULAR BONE
- CUBOID BONE
- CUNEIFORM BONE
- METATARSAL BONE
- PHALANGE
- TALUS
- CALCANEUS

-THE LARGEST BONE IN A HUMAN FOOT IS THE CALCANEUS WHILE THE SMALLEST BONE IS THE CUNEIFORMS CLOSER TO THE METATARSALS.

-THE NAVICULAR BONE IS RESPONSIBLE FOR MAINTAINING THE ARCH OF THE FOOT

-PHALANGE BONES PLAY VERY IMPORTANT ROLE ALLOWING YOUR TOES TO BEND PROPERLY

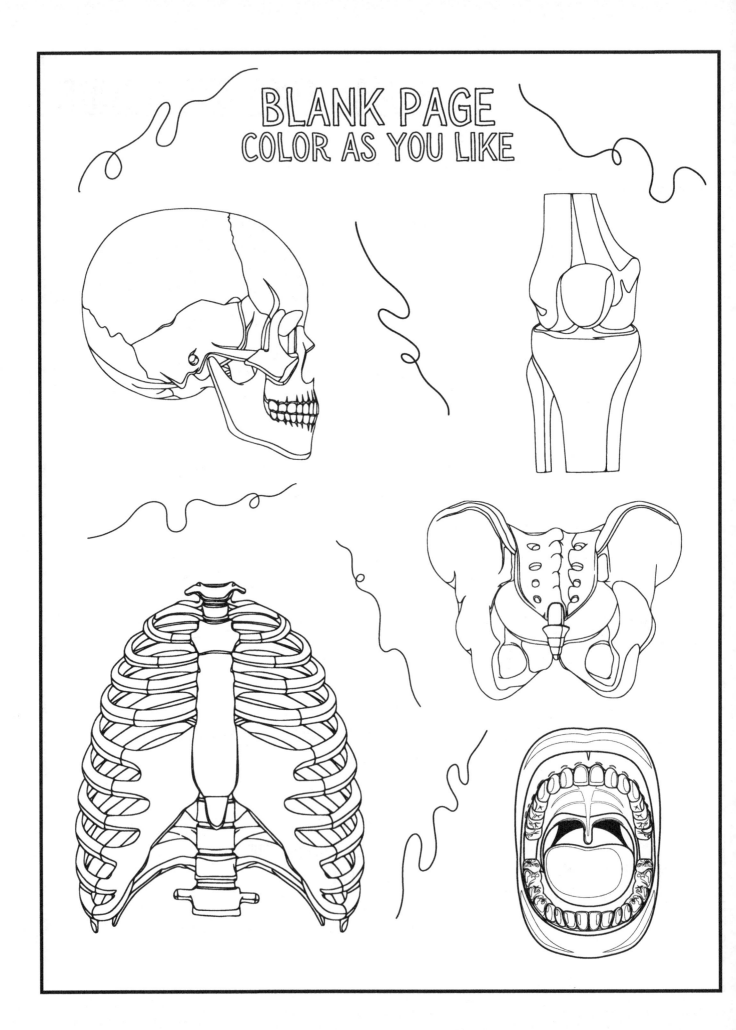

BONE ANATOMY

- THE EPIPHYSIS CONTAINS SPONGY TISSUES WHICH PRODUCE RED AND WHITE BLOOD CELLS

THE DIAPHYSIS IS THE SHAFT OF THE BONE. ITS FUNCTION IS TO BE RIGID ENOUGH TO TOLERATE STRONG FORCES AND NOT BREAK OR BEND.

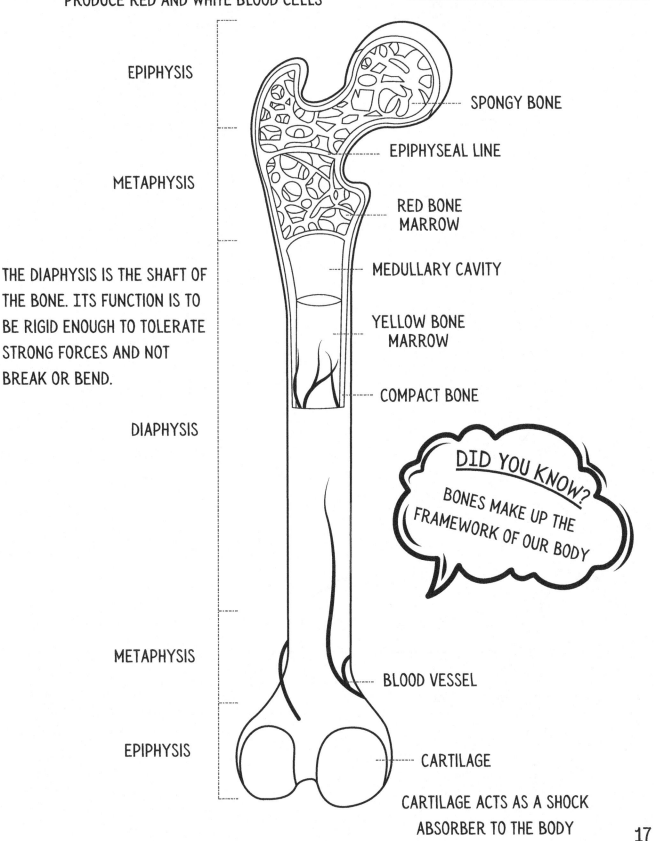

EPIPHYSIS

METAPHYSIS

DIAPHYSIS

METAPHYSIS

EPIPHYSIS

SPONGY BONE

EPIPHYSEAL LINE

RED BONE MARROW

MEDULLARY CAVITY

YELLOW BONE MARROW

COMPACT BONE

BLOOD VESSEL

CARTILAGE

DID YOU KNOW? BONES MAKE UP THE FRAMEWORK OF OUR BODY

CARTILAGE ACTS AS A SHOCK ABSORBER TO THE BODY

17

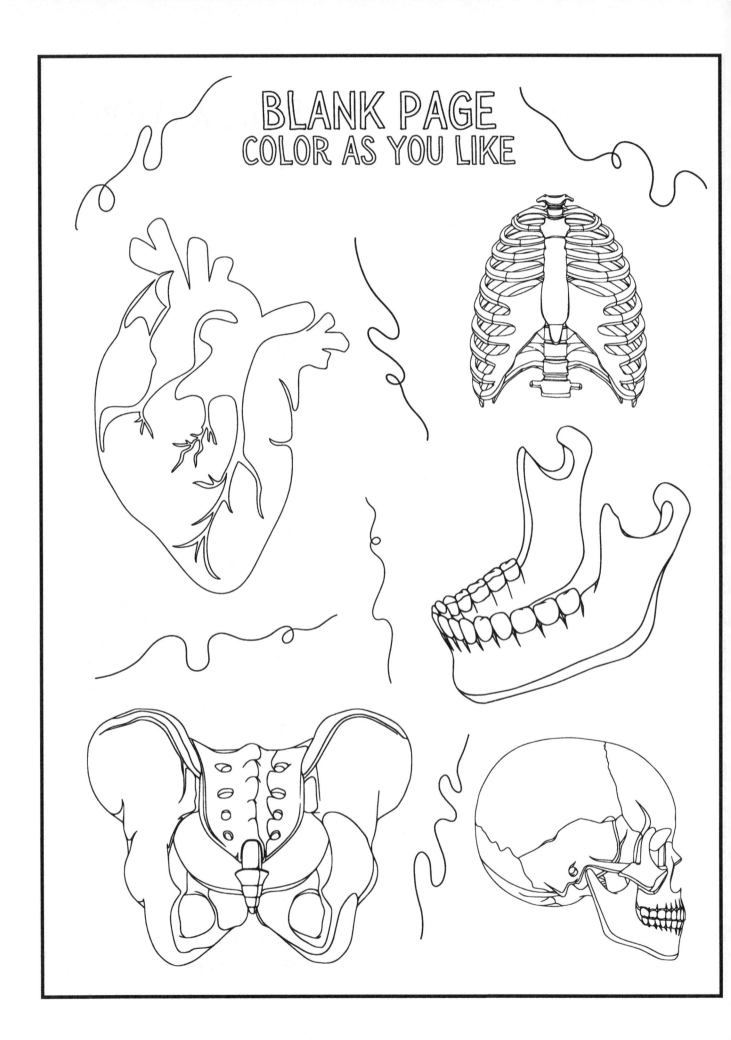

UPPER BODY MUSCLES

- ALL MOVEMENTS IN THE BODY ARE CONTROLLED BY MUSCLES.

- MUSCLES WORK BY EITHER RELAXING OR CONTRACTING TO CAUSE MOVEMENT.

- THIS MOVEMENT MAY BE VOLUNTARY (CONSCIOUSLY DONE) LIKE WALKING, LIFTING WEIGHTS, OR INVOLUNTARILY (UNCONSCIOUSLY)

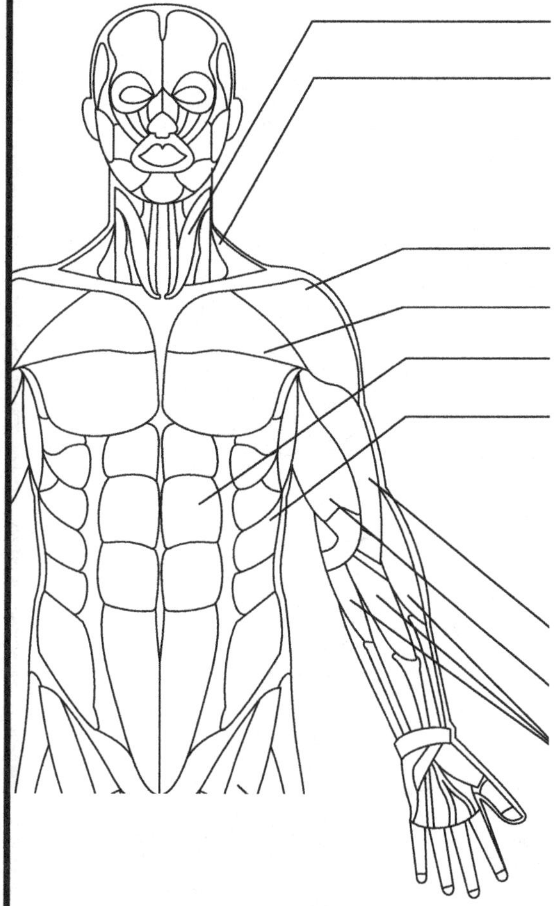

Front view labels:
- STERNOCLEIDOMASTOID
- TRAPEZIUS
- DELTOID
- PECTORALIS MAJOR
- RECTUS ABDOMINIS
- EXTERNAL OBLIQUE
- TRICEPS BRACHII
- BICEPS BRACHII
- FINGER FLEXORS

DID YOU KNOW?
THERE ARE ROUGHLY 600 MUSCLES IN THE HUMAN BODY

Back view labels:
- TRAPEZIUS
- DELTOID
- LATISSIMUS DORSI
- TRICEPS BRACHII
- FINGER EXTENSORS

- TRAPEZIUS MUSCLE FUNCTION IS TO STABILIZE AND MOVE THE SCAPULA

- DELTOID IS THE MUSCLE RESPONSIBLE FOR THE ARM ABDUCTION, WHICH MEANS RAISING YOUR ARM OUT

- THE LATISSIMUS DORSI, ALSO KNOWN AS LATS IS THE WIDEST MUSCLE IN YOUR BODY

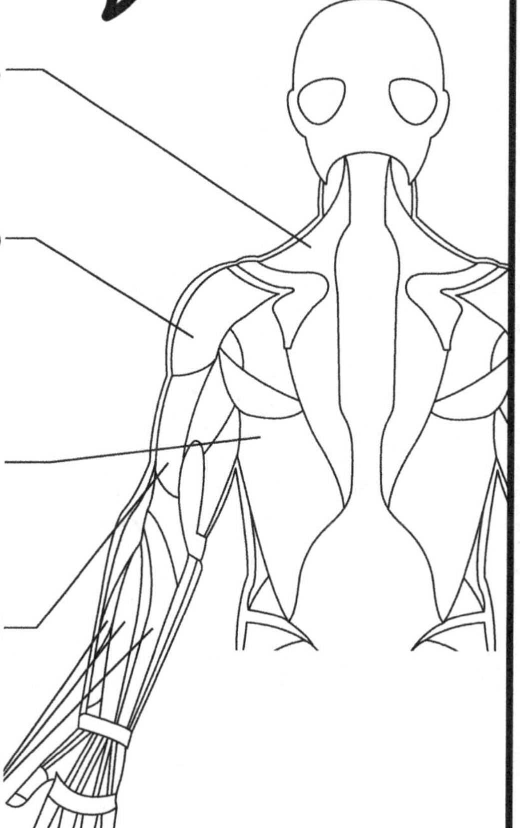

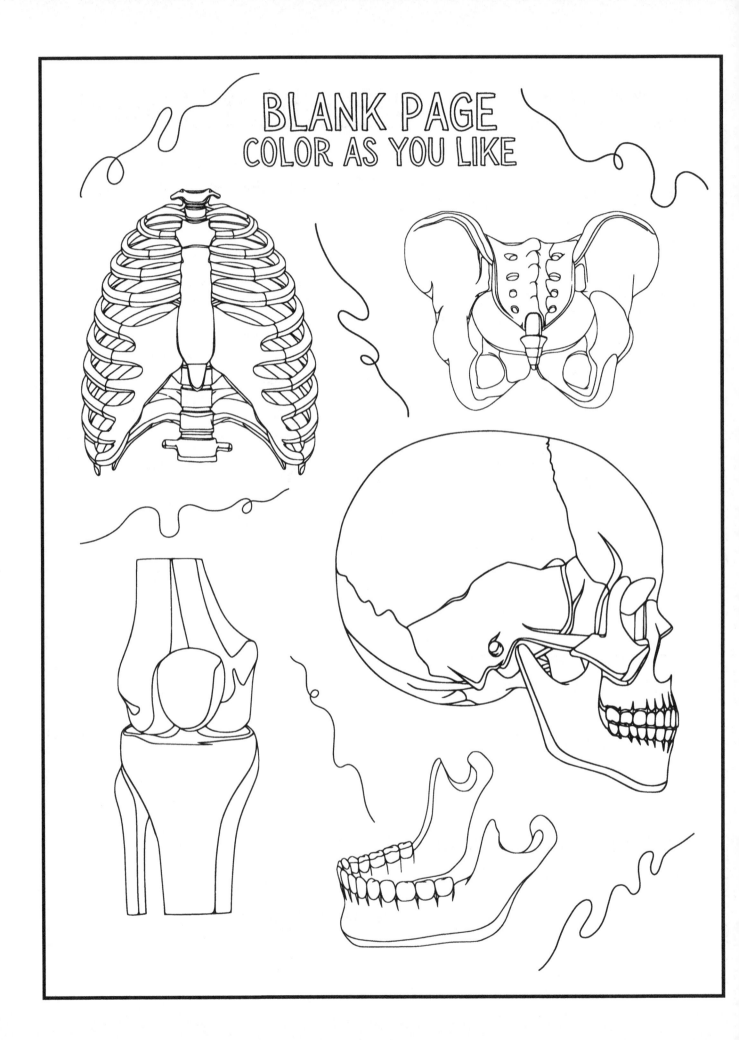

LOWER BODY MUSCLES

DID YOU KNOW?
THE AVERAGE PERSON TAKES BETWEEN 6,000 AND 9,000 STEPS EVERY DAY

- THE ADDUCTOR LONGUS MUSCLE ROTATES AND FLEXES THE THIGH.

SARTORIUS
ADDUCTOR LONGUS
RECTUS FEMORIS

- RECTUS FEMORIS MUSCLE IS RESPONSIBLE FOR KNEE EXTENSION

GLUTEUS MAXIMUS

- THE GLUTEUS MAXIMUS WORKS WITH THE SEMIMEMBRANOSUS MUSCLE AND IS RESPONSIBLE FOR THE HIP EXTENSION

SEMIMEMBRANOSUS
BICEPS FEMORIS

- THE BICEPS FEMORIS MUSCLE IS RESPONSIBLE FOR KNEE FLECTION

GASTROCNEMIUS
SOLEUS

- THE GASTROCNEMIUS AND THE SOLEUS ARE THE TWO MOST IMPORTNAT ANKLE JOINT FLEXORS.

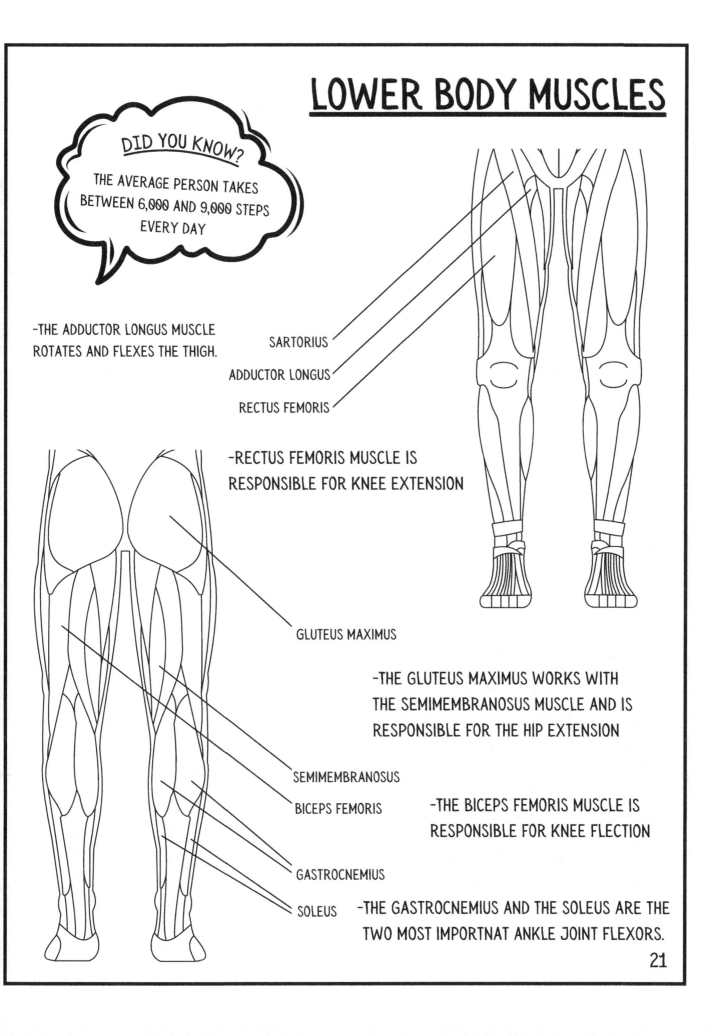

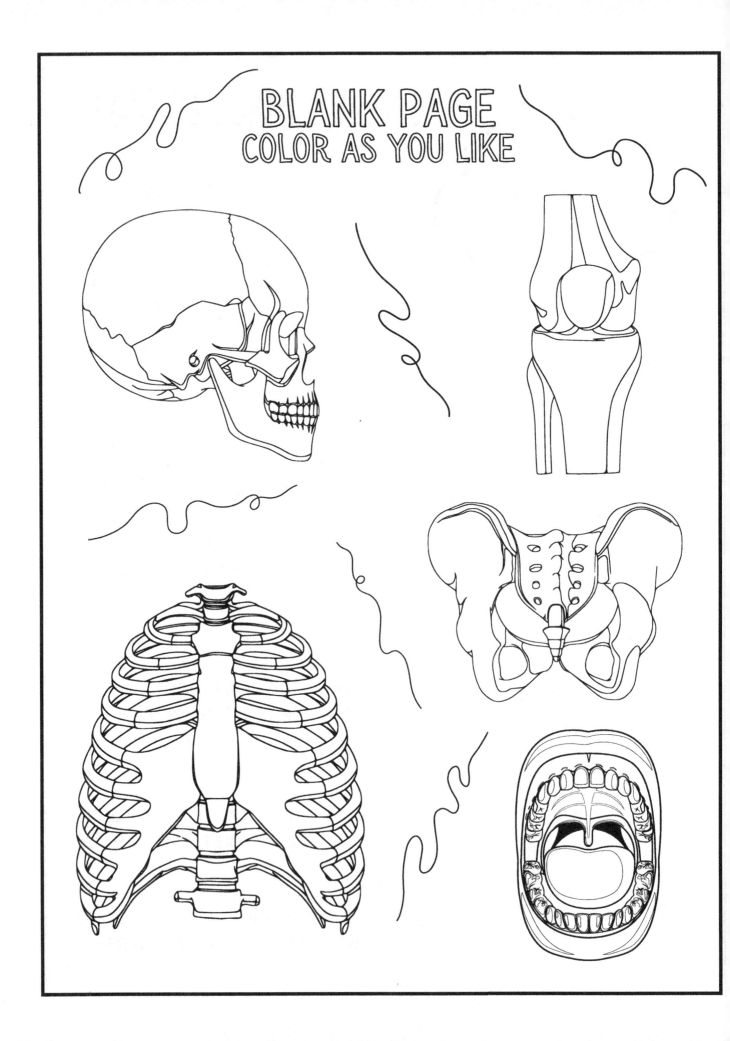

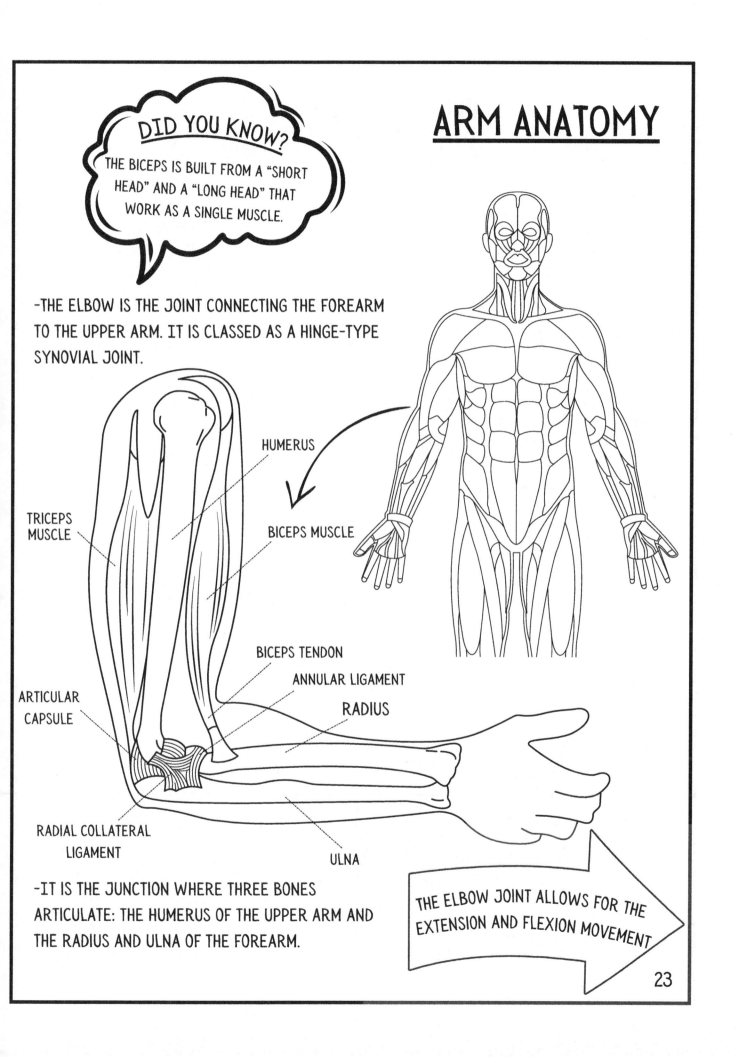

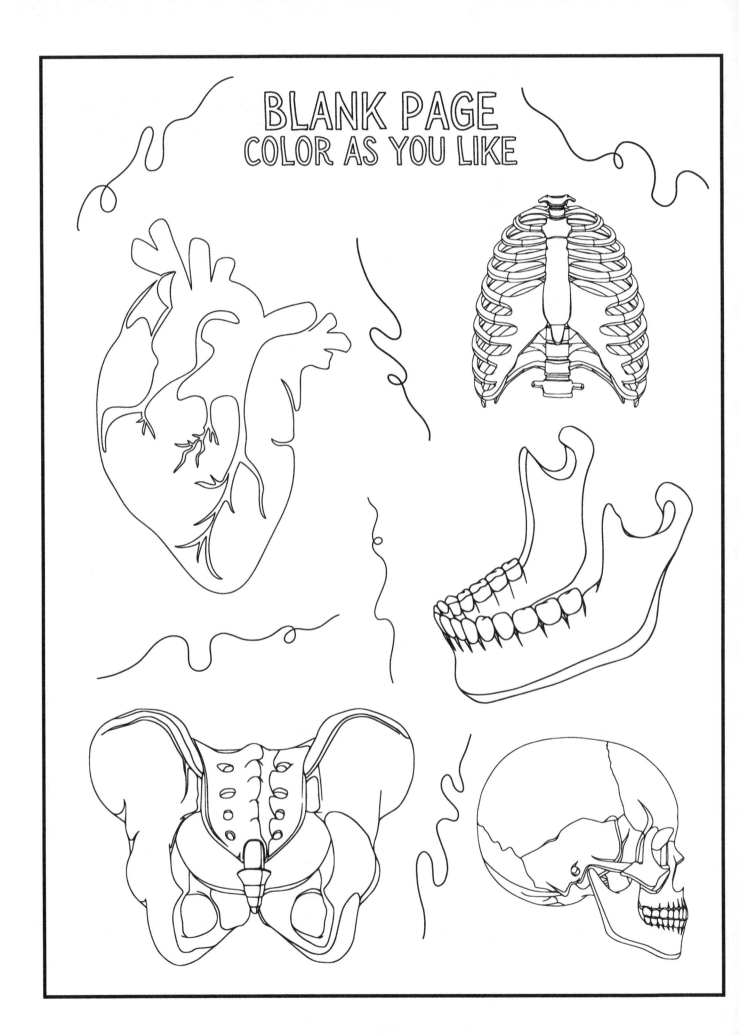

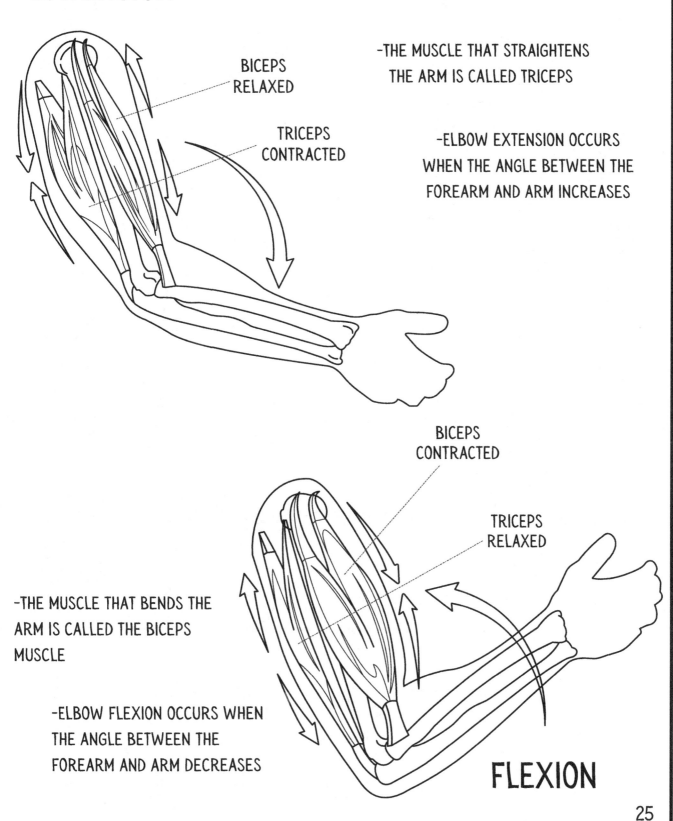

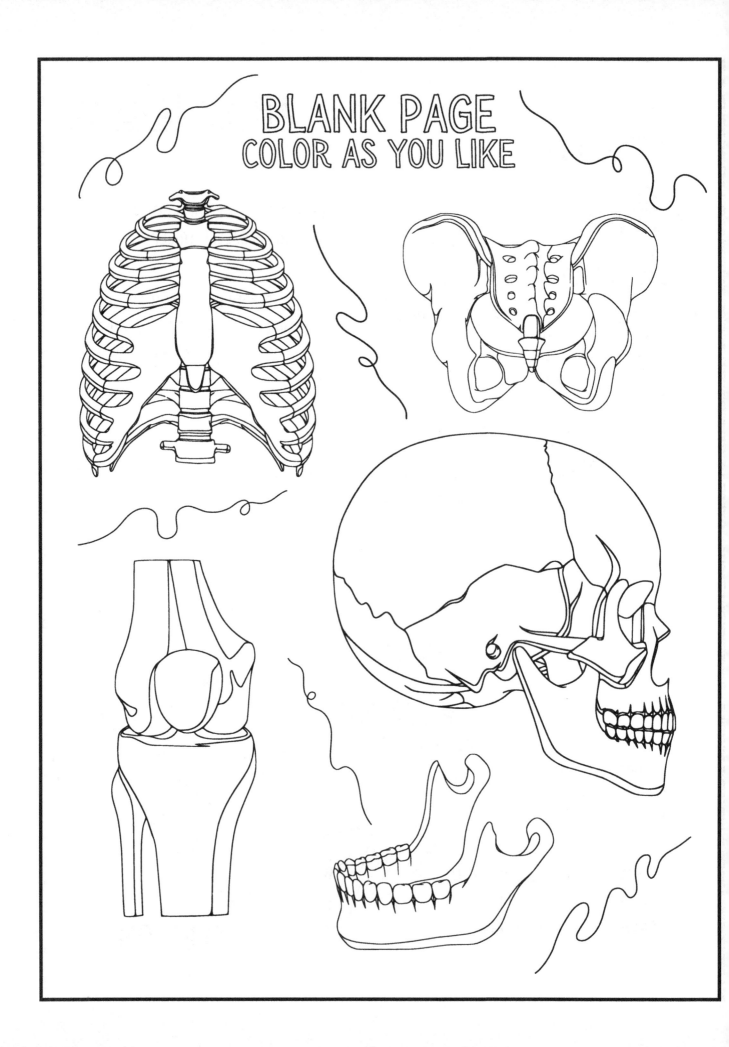

BRAIN ANATOMY

- THE BRAIN IS THE CONTROL CENTER OF THE BODY RESPONSIBLE FOR ALL THE ACTIVITIES IN THE BODY. IT CONTROLS MEMORY, EMOTION, TOUCH, VISION, HUNGER, TEMPERATURE, BREATHING

- THE BRAIN WEIGHS ABOUT 3 POUNDS AND IT DECREASES WITH AGE

FRONTAL LOBE
- PROBLEM SOLVING
- PLANNING
- SPEAKING
- PERSONALITY
- CONCENTRATION

PARETIAL LOBE
- CALCULATIONS
- READING
- WRITING
- TOUCH
- TASTE
- SMELL

OCCIPITAL LOBE
- VISUAL INTERPRETATION

CEREBELLUM
- COORDINATION
- BALANCE
- MUSCLE MEMORY

BRAIN STEM
- BREATHING
- HEART CONTROL
- DIGESTION
- HEART RATE
- SWALLOWING

TEMPORAL LOBE
- MEMORY
- HEARING
- LEARNING
- FEELINGS

DID YOU KNOW? BRAIN'S STORAGE CAPACITY IS CONSIDERED UNLIMITED.

- ALL THE PARTS OF THE BRAIN WORK TOGETHER, BUT EACH PART HAS ITS OWN SPECIAL DUTIES.

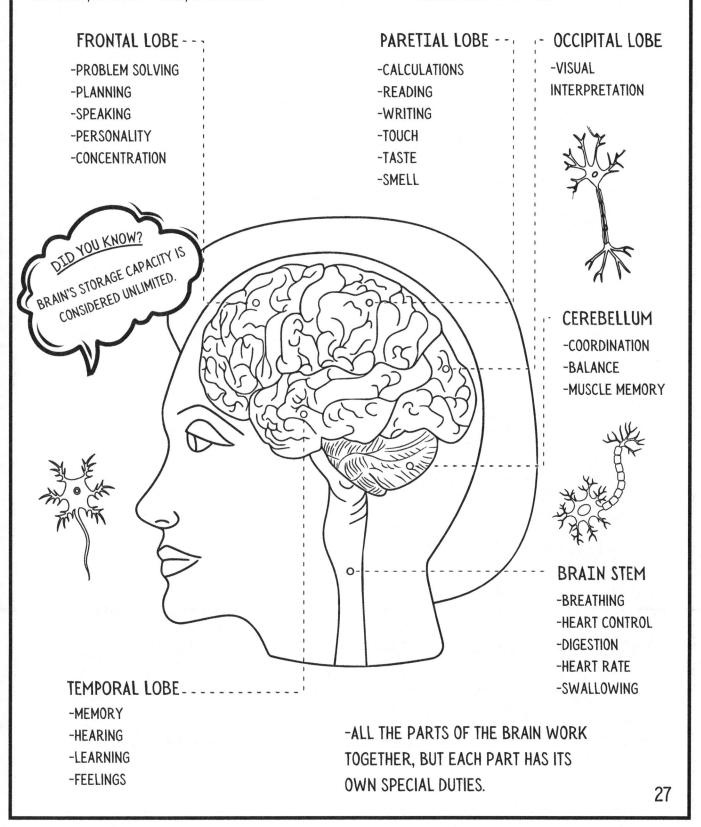

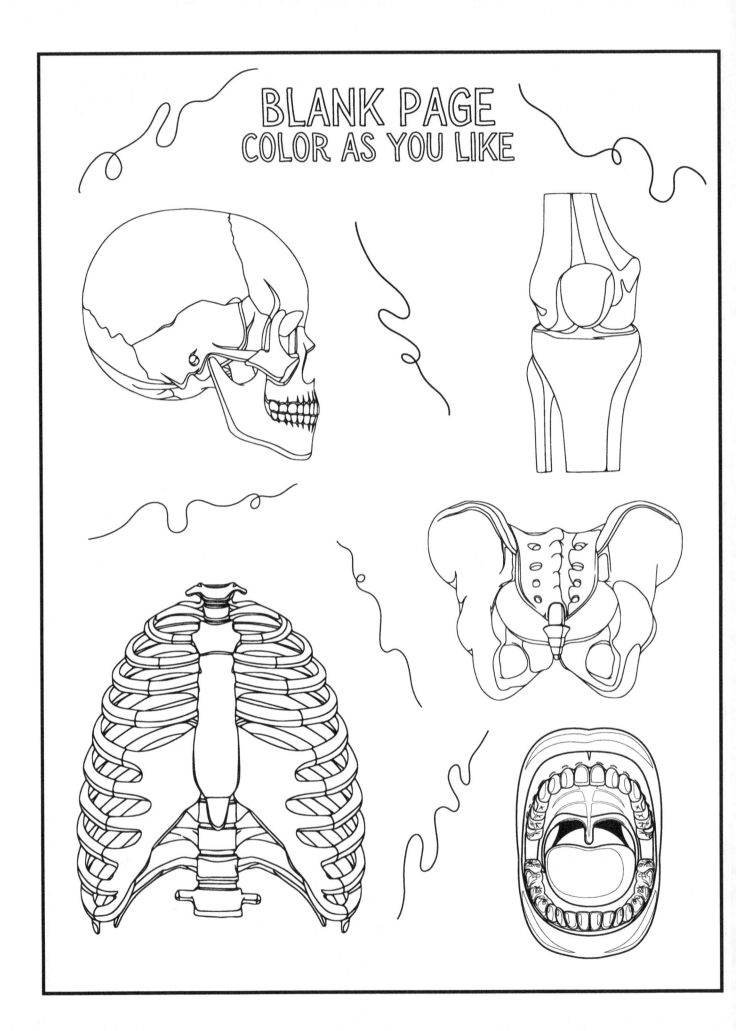

EYE ANATOMY

DID YOU KNOW? HUMAN EYES CAN DISTINGUISH APPROXIMATELY 10 MILLION DIFFERENT COLORS.

THE EYE IS THE ORGAN FOR SIGHT.

- THE SCLERA IS THE WHITE PART OF THE EYE.

- PUPIL - THE PUPILS IS THE DARK MIDDLE CIRCLE SURROUNDED BY THE IRIS. IT ALLOWS LIGHT TO ENTER YOUR EYE.

- IRIS- THE IRIS IS THE COLORED PART OF THE EYE. IT COULD BE BLACK, BLUE, BROWN, OR GREEN

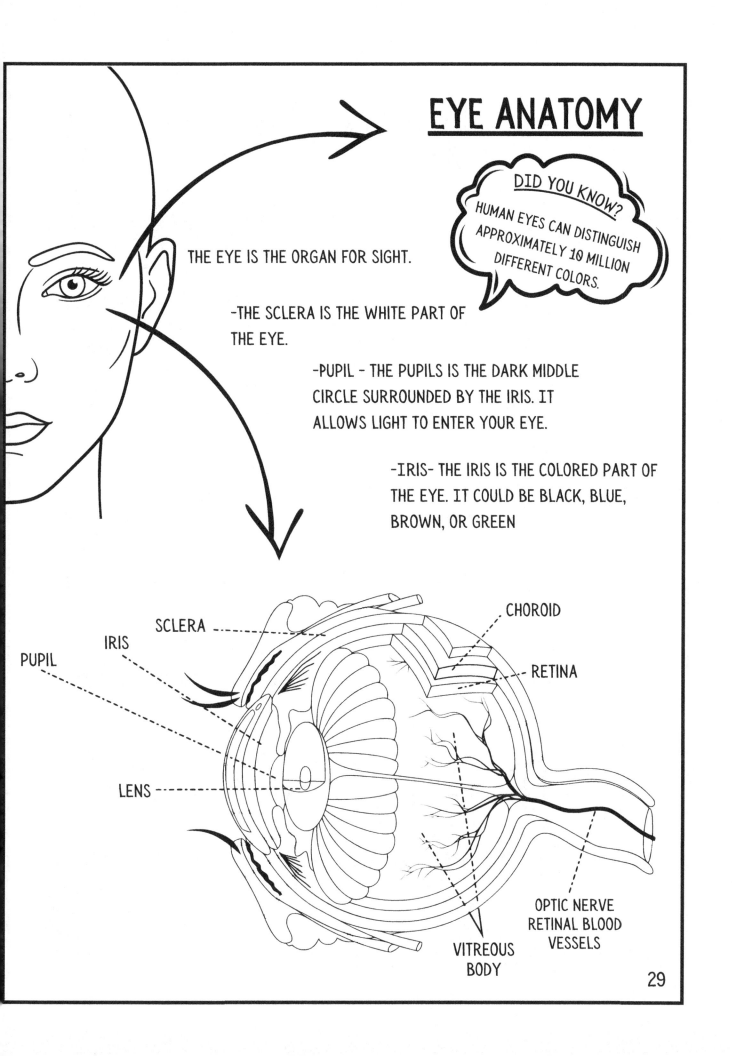

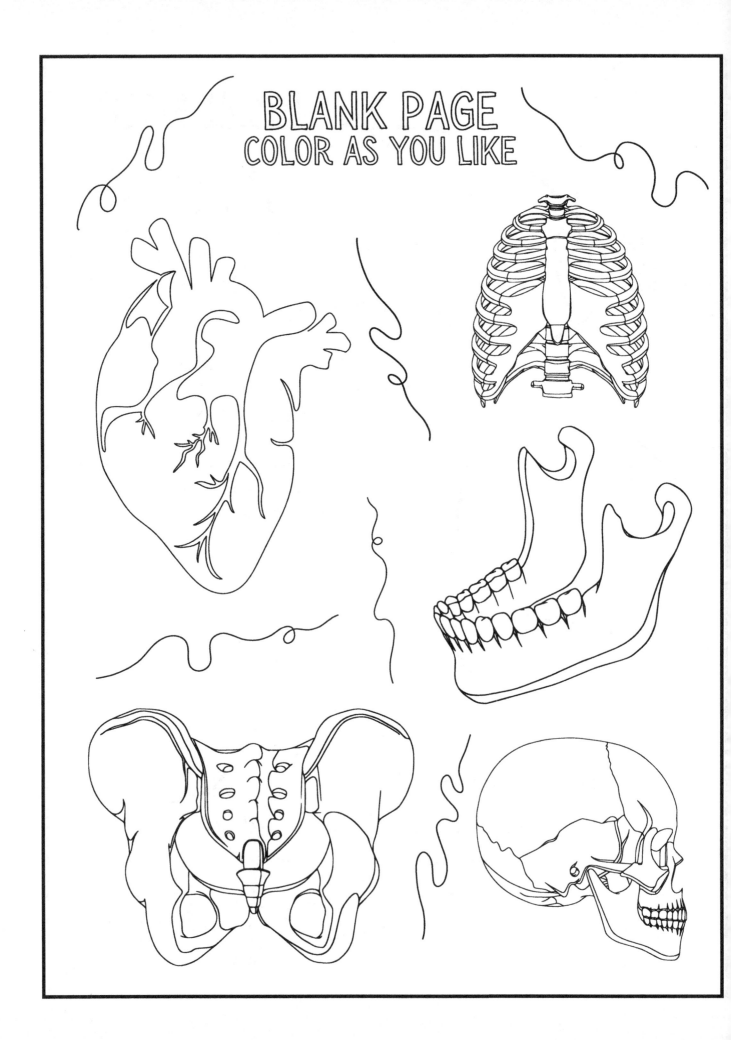

EAR ANATOMY

-THE EAR IS THE ORGAN OF HEARING AND BALANCE.

1. THE VISIBLE PART OF THE EAR IS CALLED PINNA. IT COLLECTS SOUND AND TRANSFERS IT TO THE EAR CANAL

2. THE SOUND TRAVELS TO THE EARDRUM CAUSING IT TO VIBRATE.

3. THE VIBRATIONS SET THE MALLEUS, INCUS AND STAPES INTO MOTION AND AMPLIFY THE SOUND

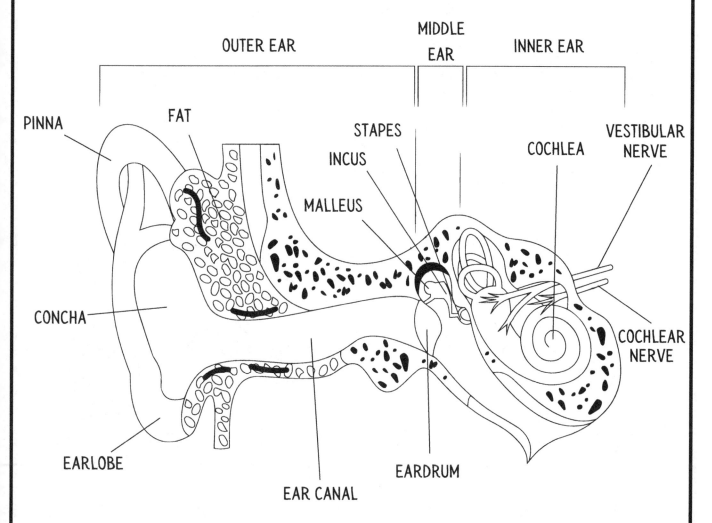

4. THE SOUND WAVES INTO THE COCHLEA, A SNAIL-SHAPED ORGAN WHICH CONTAINS FLUID THAT MOVES FROM THE VIBRATIONS. THE FLUID ACTIVATES NERVE ENDINGS THAT TRANSFORM THE VIBRATIONS INTO ELECTRICAL IMPULSES. THE IMPULSES ARE BEING INTERPRETED BY BRAIN AND THIS IS WHAT WE HEAR

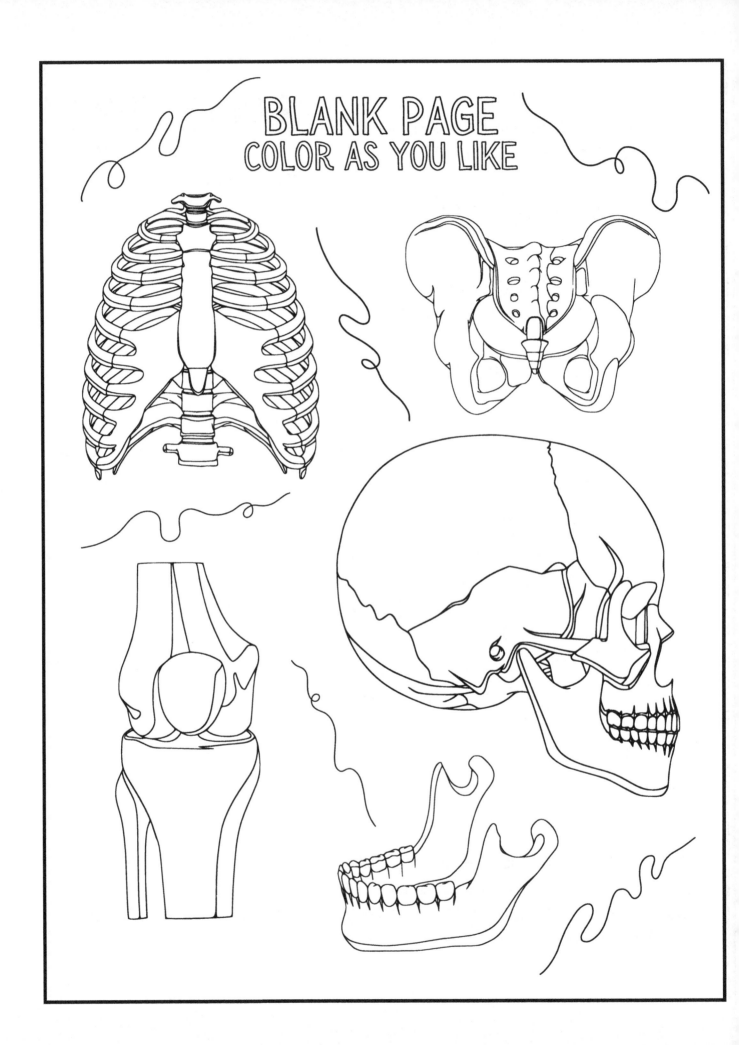

MOUTH ANATOMY

- THE MOUTH IS ALSO KNOWN AS THE ORAL OR BUCCAL CAVITY. IT IS ESSENTIAL FOR ACTIVITIES LIKE SPEAKING AND EATING

- THE LIP IS THE ENTRANCE TO THE MOUTH AND ARE MADE UP OF MUSCLE, SKIN AND MUCOUS MEMBRANES. THE GUM HUGS THE TEETH.

- THE UVULA FUNCTION IS TO SECRET LARGE AMOUNTS OF SALIVA THAT KEEP YOUR THROAT MOIST AND LUBRICATED.

- THE TONSILS FILTER OUT GERMS THAT ENTER THROUGH YOUR MOUTH AND PROTECT BODY FROM INFECTION.

- THE DIGESTION PROCESS STARTS FROM THE MOUTH. THE FOOD IS GROUND BY THE TEETH WHILE THE SALIVA HAS AN ENZYME THAT HELPS BREAKDOWN THE FOOD. THE HARD PALATE IS THE ROOF OF THE MOUTH.

Labels: LIP, GUM, HARD PALATE, UVULA, TONSILS, TONGUE

DID YOU KNOW? WE PRODUCE AROUND 38 000 LITRES OF SALIVA DURING OUR LIVES

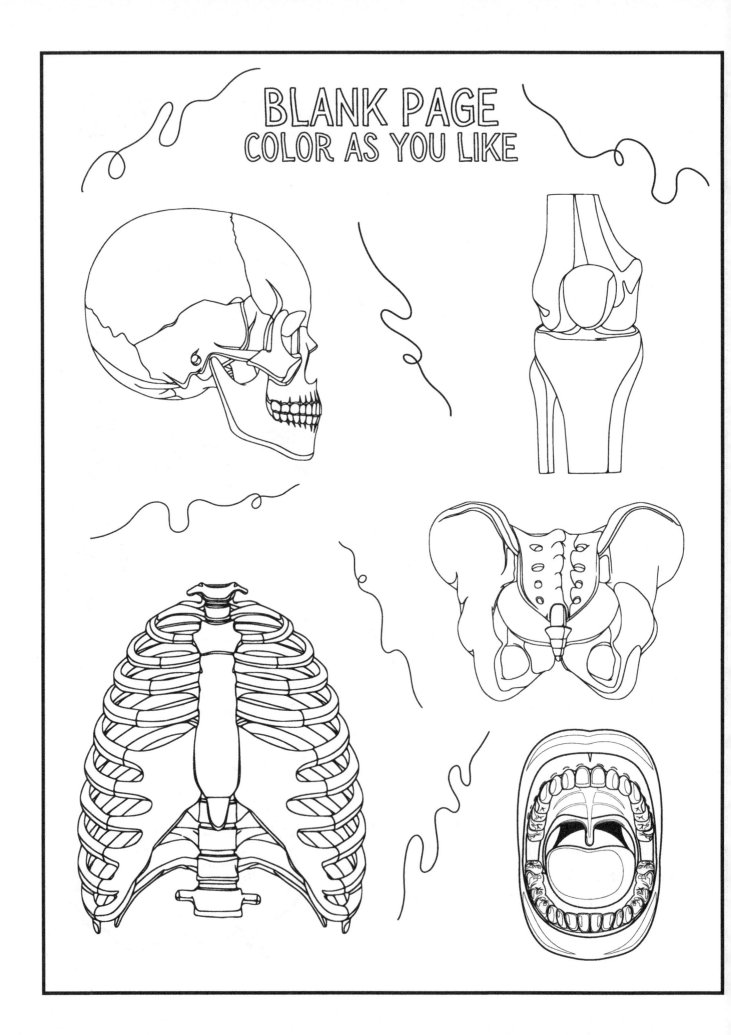

AT BIRTH, YOU HAVE 20 BABY TEETH THAT START TO DEVELOP AT 6 MONTHS OF AGE BUT ADULT MOUTH CONSISTS OF 32 TEETH.

HUMAN TEETH

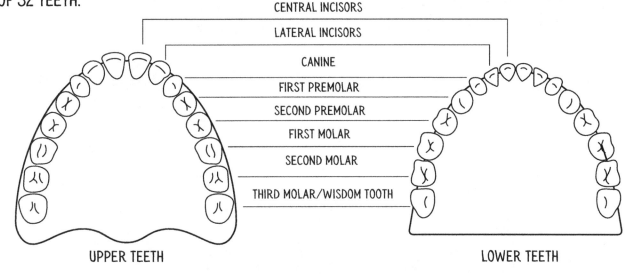

THERE ARE FOUR DIFFERENT TYPES OF TEETH

-INCISORS - THEY ARE 8 IN NUMBER AND LOCATED AT THE FRONT AND HELP CUT FOOD

-CANINES - POINTY AND SHARP TEETH ON EACH SIDE USED FOR TEARING AND HOLDING FOOD. THEY ARE USUALLY FOUR IN NUMBER.

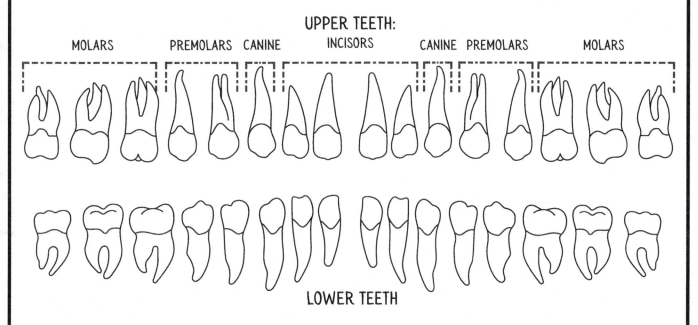

-PREMOLARS - THEY ARE LOCATED BETWEEN THE MOLARS AND CANINES

-MOLARS - THEY ARE LOCATED AT THE BACK OF THE MOUTH TO HELP CHEW, CRUSH AND GRIND FOOD BEFORE SWALLOWING

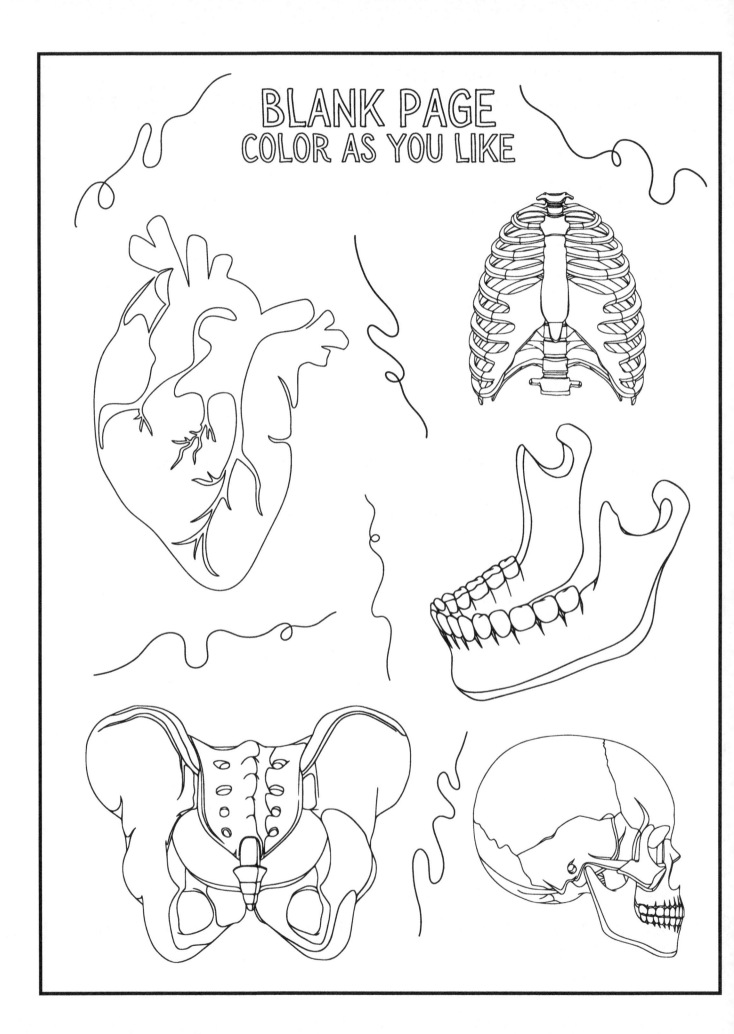

TOOTH STRUCTURE

CROWN

NECK

ROOT

SEVERAL LAYERS MAKE UP A TOOTH
- THE VISIBLE PART IS CALLED THE CROWN.

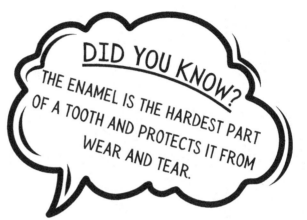

DID YOU KNOW?
THE ENAMEL IS THE HARDEST PART OF A TOOTH AND PROTECTS IT FROM WEAR AND TEAR.

- THE DENTIN MAKES UP THE LARGEST PART OF THE TOOTH.

- THE PULP IS A SOFT TISSUE THAT CONTAINS NERVES AND BLOOD.

- THE GUM IS A SOFT TISSUE AROUND THE BASE OF EACH TOOTH.
- THE ROOTS OF THE TEETH LIE BELOW THE GUMS.

- CEMENTUM IS A GLUELIKE SUBSTANCE THAT KEEPS THE TEETH STUCK IN THE JAWBONE.

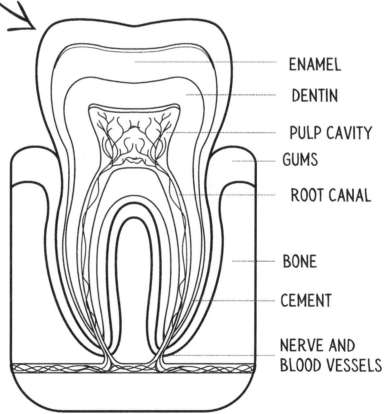

37

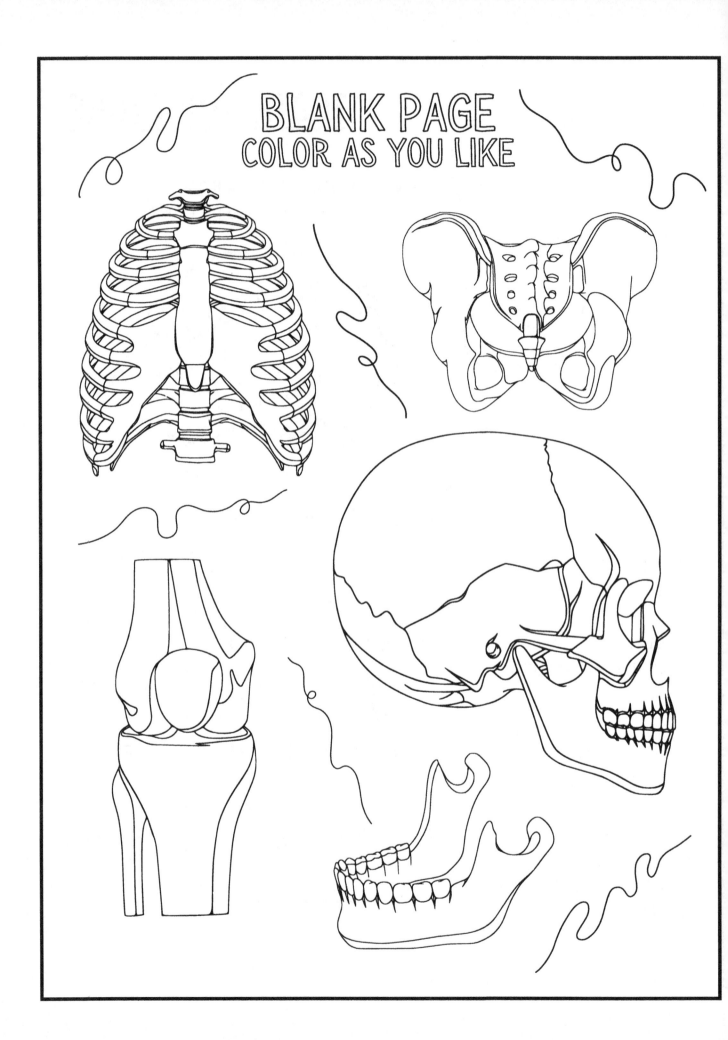

HUMAN TONGUE

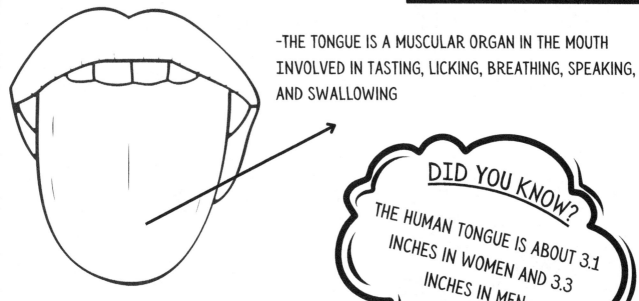

-THE TONGUE IS A MUSCULAR ORGAN IN THE MOUTH INVOLVED IN TASTING, LICKING, BREATHING, SPEAKING, AND SWALLOWING

DID YOU KNOW?
THE HUMAN TONGUE IS ABOUT 3.1 INCHES IN WOMEN AND 3.3 INCHES IN MEN

THE TONGUE HAS 5 TASTE BUDS NAMELY SOUR, UMAMI, SALTY, SWEET, AND BITTER:

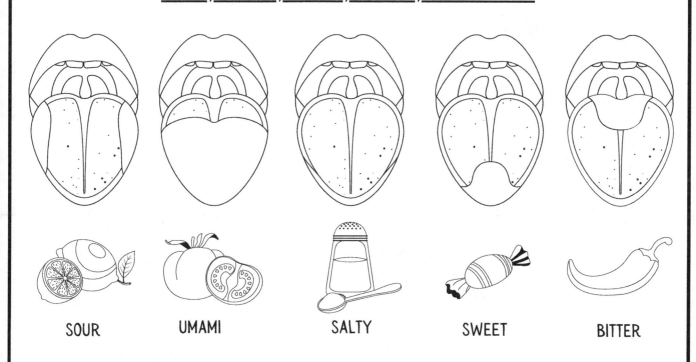

SOUR | UMAMI | SALTY | SWEET | BITTER

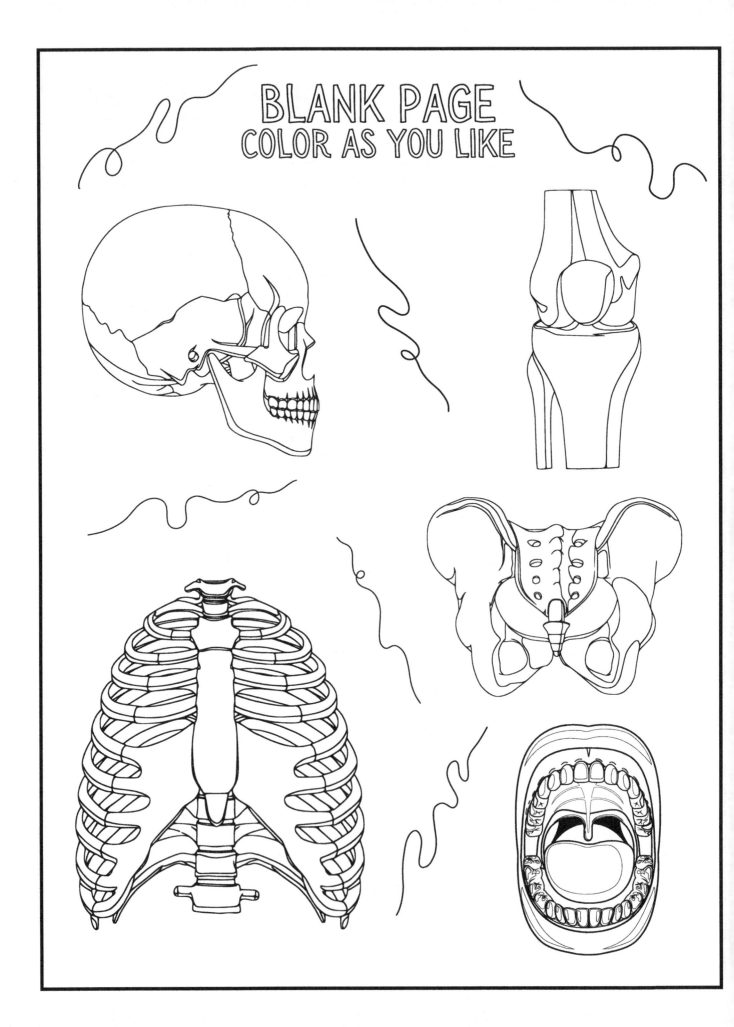

DIGESTIVE SYSTEM

DIGESTIVE SYSTEM IS STRUCTURE OF ORGANS THAT TAKES IN FOOD AND LIQUIDS TO BREAK THEM DOWN INTO SUBSTANCES THAT THE BODY USES FOR GROWTH AND ENERGY

-THE UVULA IS ELEVATED TO PREVENT FOOD FROM ENTERING THE NASOPHARYNX

-THE PHARYNX IS THE CAVITY BEHIND THE MOUTH. FOOD IS FORCED BY THE TONGUE INTO THE PHARYNX

DID YOU KNOW? THE AVERAGE PERSON PRODUCES 32 OUNCES OF SALIVA EACH DAY. THAT IS 2 CANS OF SODA.

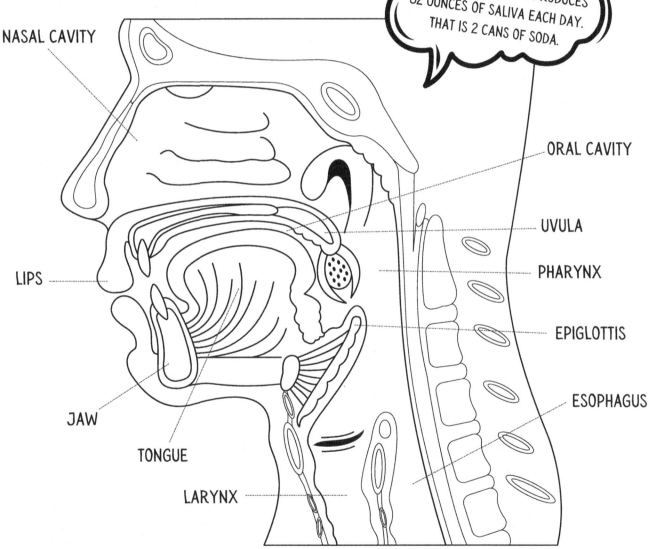

- NASAL CAVITY
- LIPS
- JAW
- TONGUE
- LARYNX
- ORAL CAVITY
- UVULA
- PHARYNX
- EPIGLOTTIS
- ESOPHAGUS

-THE EPIGLOTTIS DROPS DOWNWARD TO PREVENT FOOD FROM ENTERING THE LARYNX AND TRACHEA

-THE LARYNX IS THE UPPER PART OF THE WINDPIPE THAT CONTAINS THE VOCAL CORDS

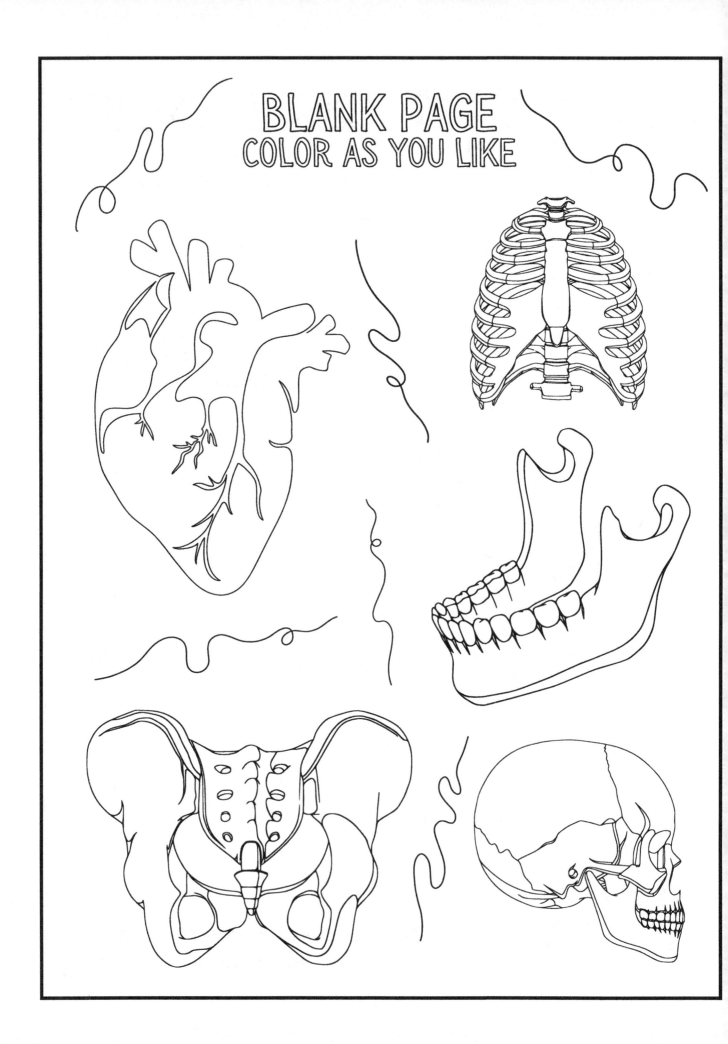

1. WHEN FOOD IS SWALLOWED FROM THE MOUTH, IT MOVES THROUGH THE ESOPHAGUS DOWN TO THE STOMACH WHERE IT IS BEEN FURTHER BROKEN DOWN INTO SMALLER PARTICLES BY ACIDS AND ENZYMES.

2. THE FOOD MOVES TO THE SMALL INTESTINE MADE UP OF THE DUODENUM, JEJUNUM, AND ILEUM. THIS IS WHERE MOST OF THE FOOD IS ABSORBED.

- LIVER
- DUODENUM
- STOMACH
- DUODENOJEJUNAL JUNCTION
- ASCENDING COLON
- CECUM
- APPENDIX
- ILEUM
- STOMACH
- PANCREAS
- LEFT COLIC FLEXURE
- TRANSVERSE COLON
- JEJUNUM
- DESCENDING COLON
- SIGMOID COLON
- RECTUM
- ANAL CANAL

3. THE LIVER AND PANCREASE RELEASE BILE AND ENZYMES THAT BREAK DOWN FAT AND OTHER FOOD PARTICLES.

4. THE LARGE INTESTINE (CECUM, ASCENDING COLON, TRANSVERSE COLON, DESCENDING COLON, AND THE SIGMOID COLON) PROCESS THE EXCRETION OF WASTE PRODUCT THROUGH THE RECTUM AND ANAL CANAL

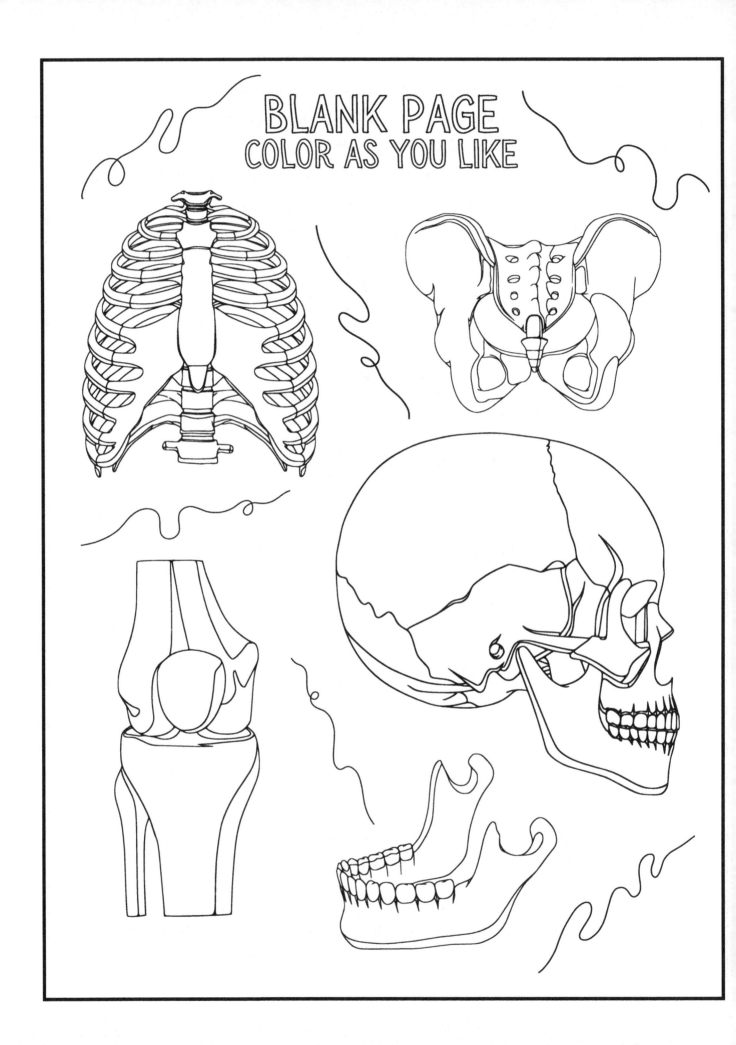

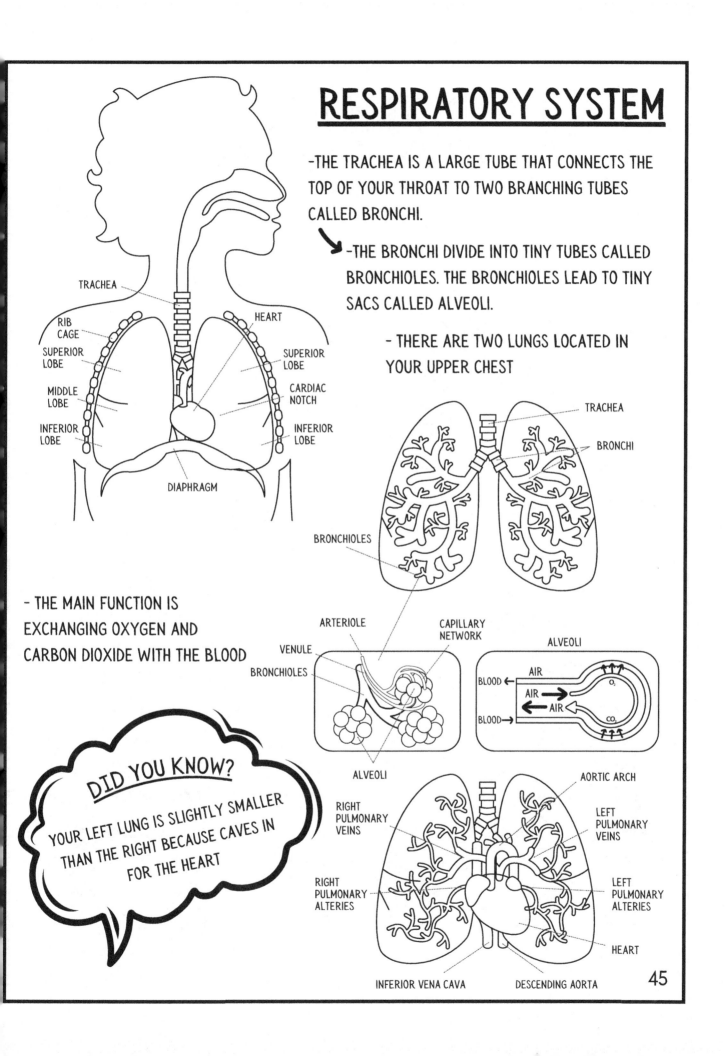

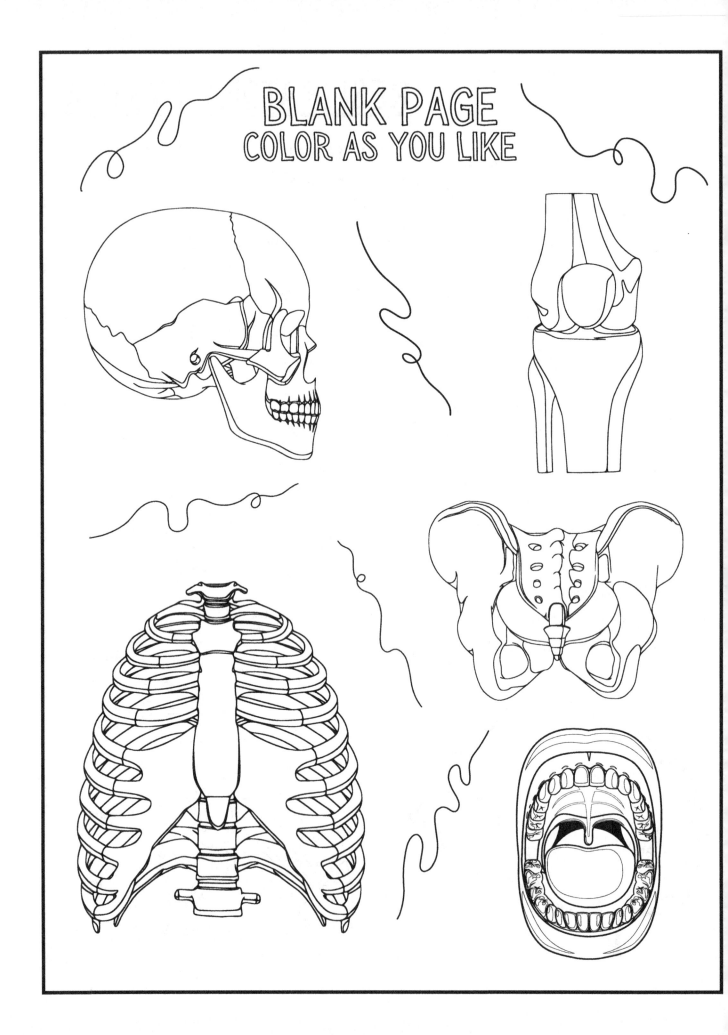

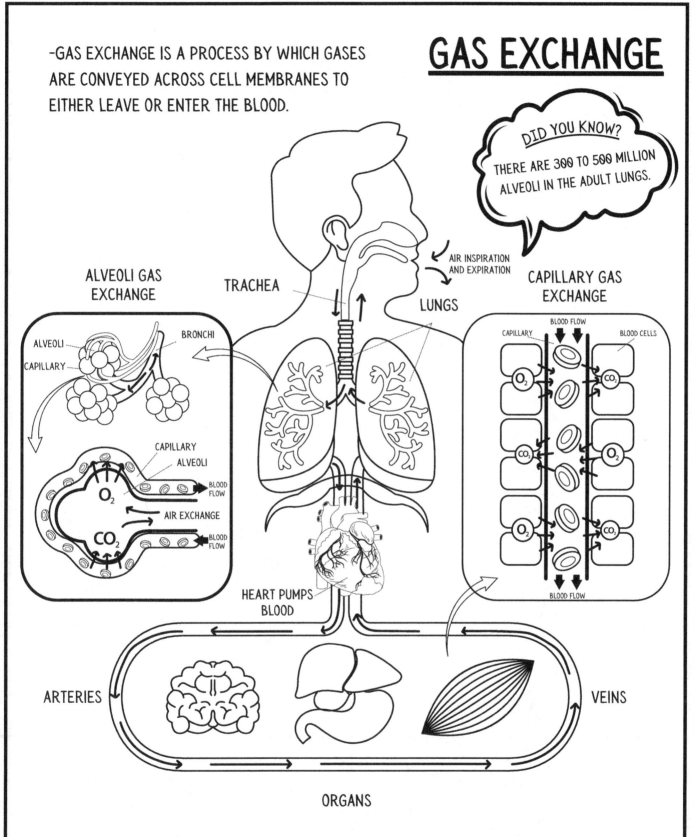

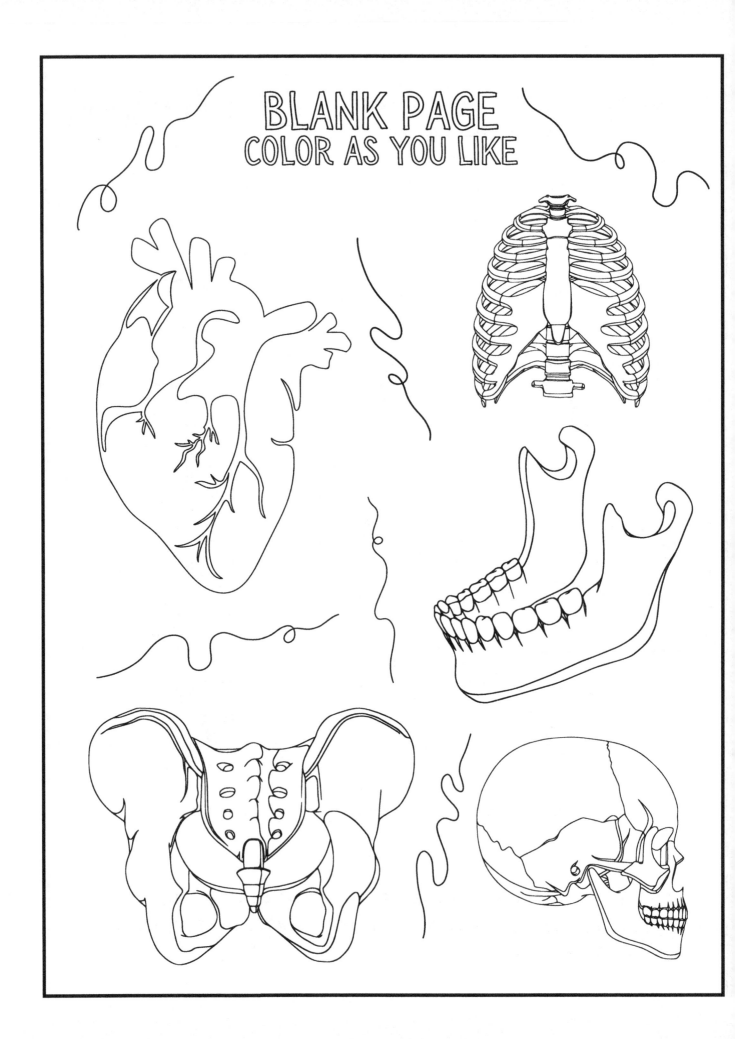

MALE REPRODUCTIVE SYSTEM

-THE MALE REPRODUCTIVE SYSTEM PRODUCES SPERM AND SENDS IT OUT OF THE BODY WHAT ALLOWS A MAN TO HAVE CHILDREN.

THIS SYSTEM IS MADE UP OF:

-THE PENIS WHICH IS MADE OF SPONGY TISSUE AND BLOOD VESSELS

-THE SCROTUM IS A SAC AT THE BASE OF THE PENIS THAT HOLDS THE TESTICLES.

DID YOU KNOW? TESTICLES ARE WHERE SPERM IS MADE.

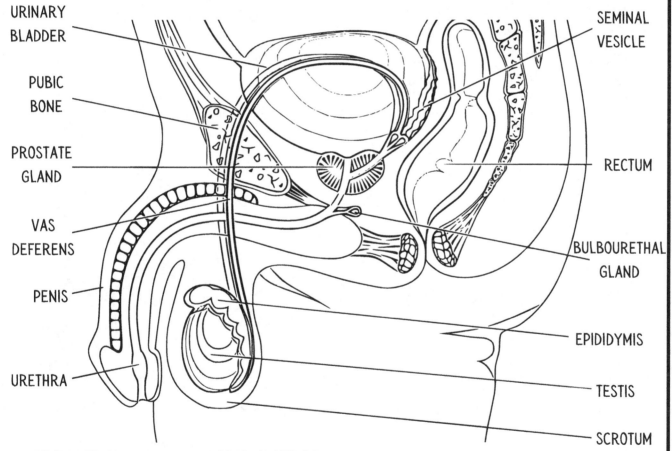

-EPIDIDYMIS ARE WHERE THE SPERM MATURE.

-SEMINAL VESICLES AND THE PROSTATE GLAND PRODUCE THE LIQUID SEMEN THAT CARRIES THE SPERM.

-THE VAS DEFERENS TUBES CARRY SEMEN TO THE URETHRA AND OUT OF THE BODY

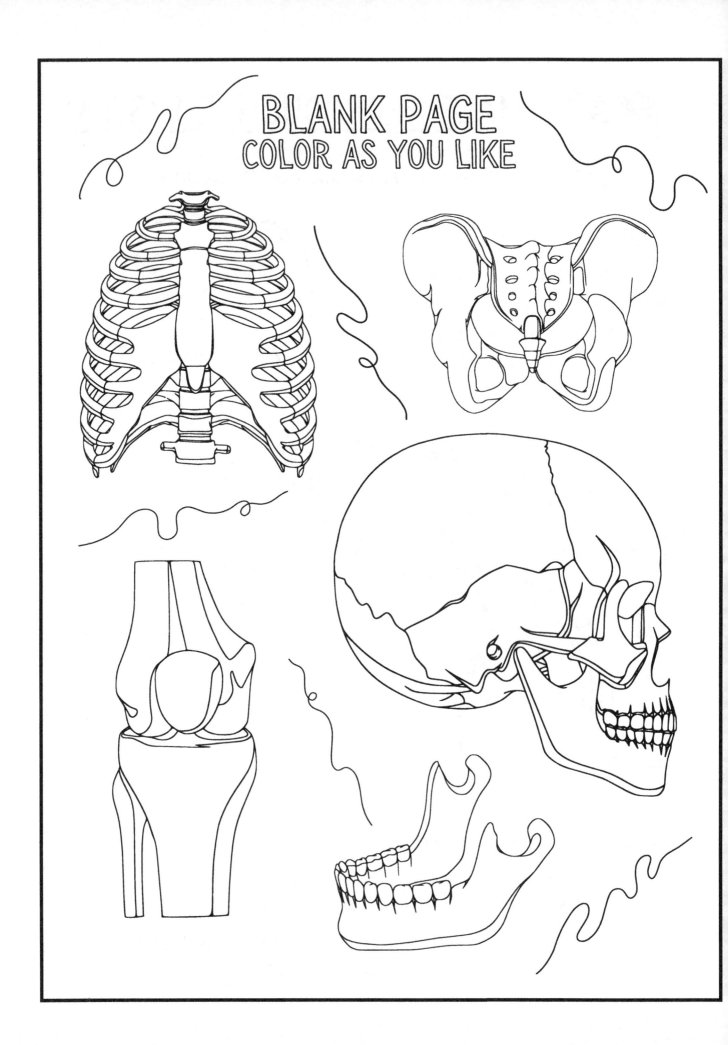

FEMALE REPRODUCTIVE SYSTEM

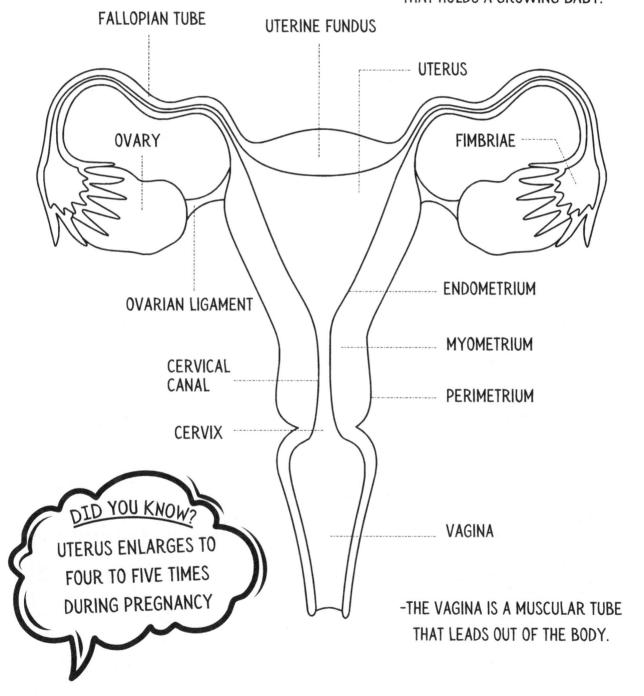

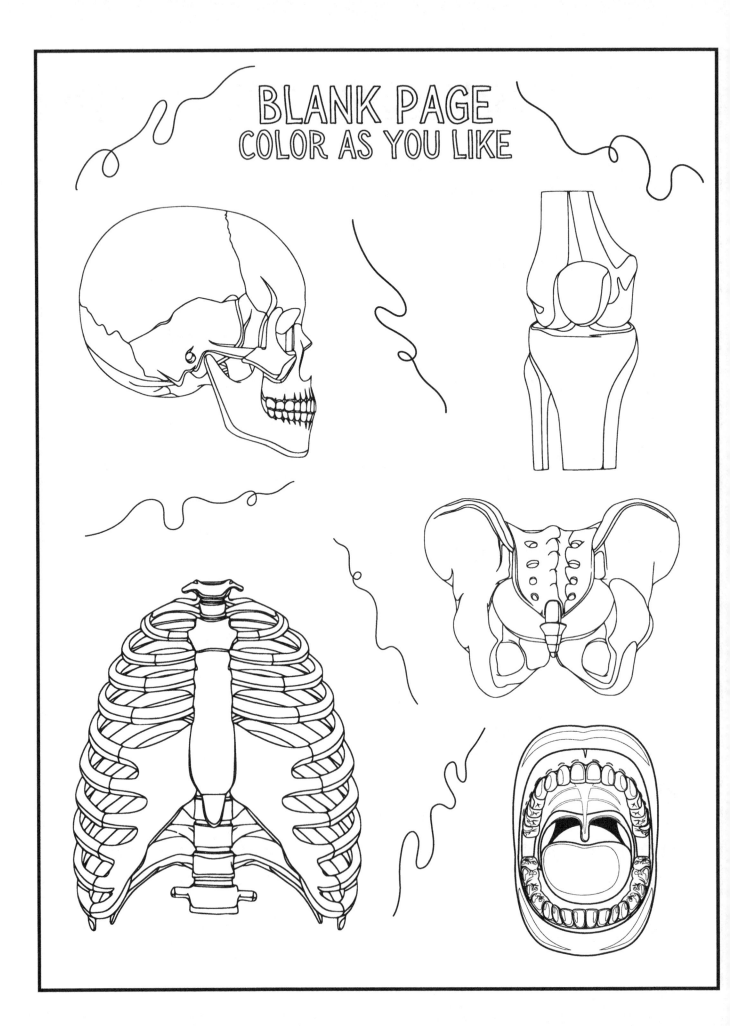

FEMALE BREAST ANATOMY

- BREASTFEEDING IS THE MAIN FUNCTION OF THE FEMALE BREAST

- THE DARK AREA OF SKIN SURROUNDING THE NIPPLE IS CALLED THE AREOLA.

DID YOU KNOW?
BREASTS ARE USUALLY ASYMETRICAL WHICH MEANS ONE IS LARGER THAN THE OTHER

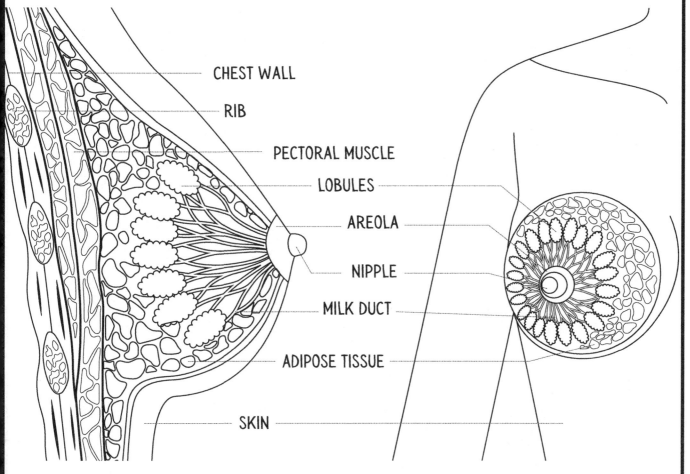

- CHEST WALL
- RIB
- PECTORAL MUSCLE
- LOBULES
- AREOLA
- NIPPLE
- MILK DUCT
- ADIPOSE TISSUE
- SKIN

- THE NIPPLE IS IN THE CENTER OF THE AREOLA AND HAS ABOUT NINE MILK DUCTS.

- THE MILK PASSES THROUGH A NETWORK OF TINY TUBES CALLED MILK DUCTS.

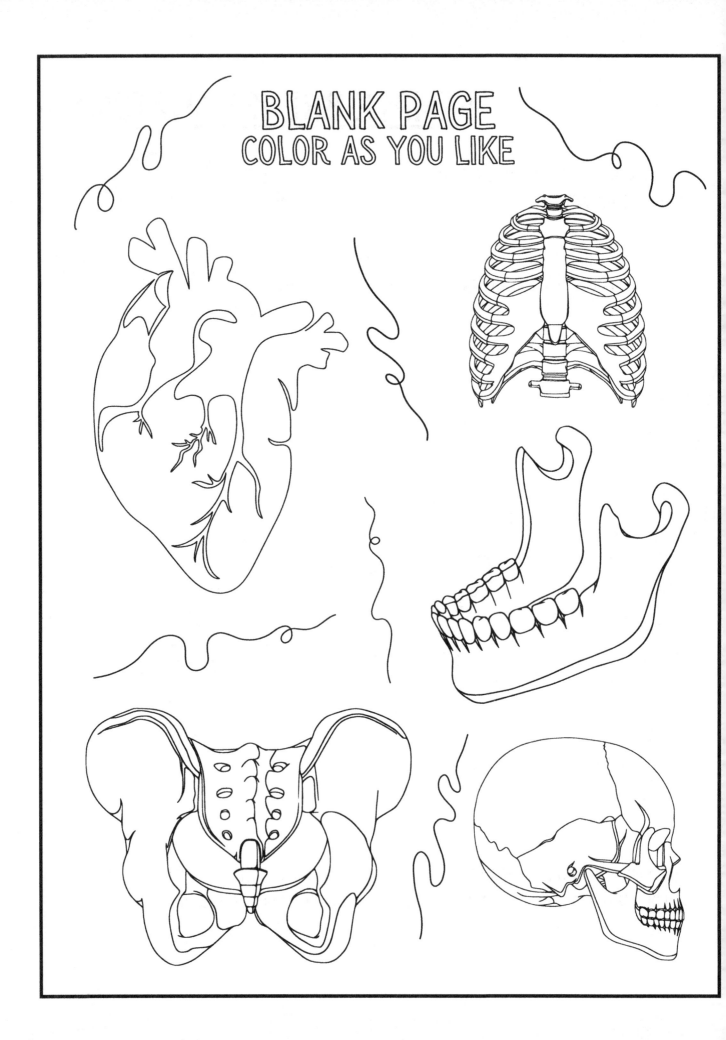

HEART ANATOMY

THE HEART IS A PEAR-SHAPED ORGAN LOCATED A LITTLE TO THE LEFT PART OF YOUR CHEST

- IT HAS FOUR CHAMBERS; LEFT ATRIUM, LEFT VENTRICLE, RIGHT ATRIUM, AND RIGHT VENTRICLE

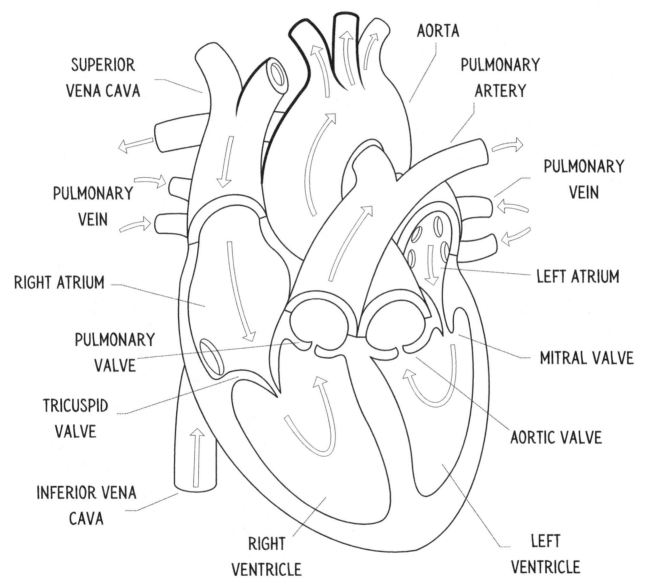

- EVERY BEAT PUMPS BLOOD TO ALL PARTS OF YOUR BODY. BLOOD CARRIES OXYGEN AND NUTRIENTS THAT THE BODY NEEDS

- AORTA CARRIES BLOOD AWAY FROM HEART TO THE REST OF YOUR BODY

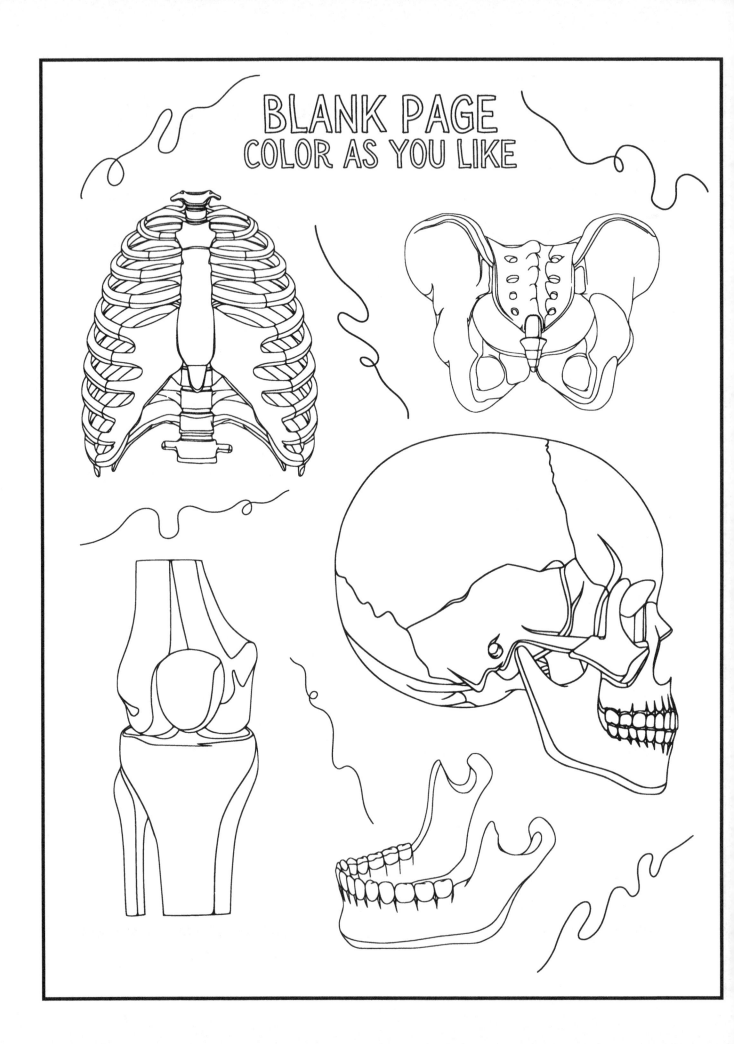

HEART BLOOD FLOW

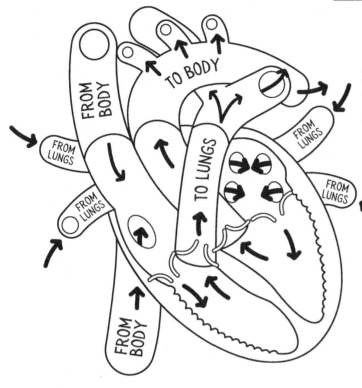

1. BLOOD FLOWS FROM THE RIGHT ATRIUM TO THE RIGHT VENTRICLE THROUGH THE TRICUSPID VALVE

2. THE RIGHT VENTRICLE PUMPS BLOOD THROUGH THE PULMONARY VALVE TO THE LUNGS TO RECEIVE OXYGEN

3. IT THEN FLOWS FROM THE LUNGS THROUGH THE PULMONARY VEINS TO THE LEFT ATRIUM

4. FROM THE LEFT ATRIUM, BLOOD FLOWS THROUGH THE MITRAL VALVE AND ENTERS THE LEFT VENTRICLE.

5. THE LEFT VENTRICLE PUMPS THE OXYGEN-RICH BLOOD TO THE REST OF THE BODY THROUGH THE AORTA.

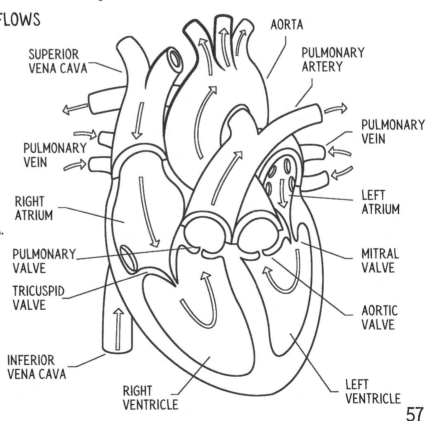

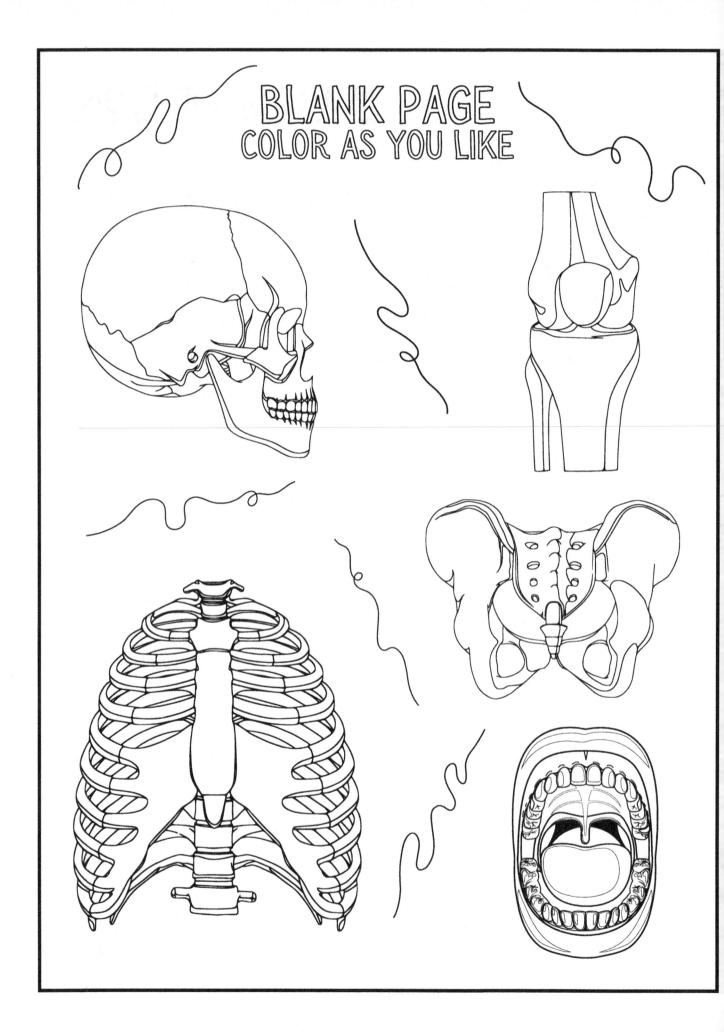

SKIN ANATOMY

DID YOU KNOW?
THE BODY RELEASES SUBSTANCES LIKE SWEAT THROUGH THE PORES. SWEAT COOLS THE BODY.

- THE SKIN IS THE LARGEST ORGAN IN THE BODY

- THE HAIR FOLLICLE RESIDES IN THE DERMAL LAYER AND REGULATES HAIR GROWTH.

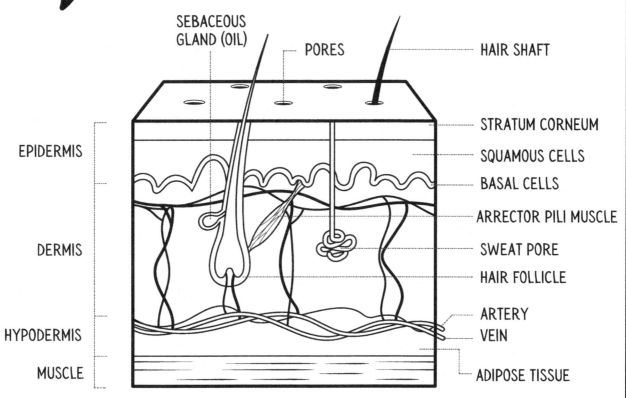

IT HAS THREE LAYERS:

- THE EPIDERMIS IS THE OUTERMOST LAYER OF SKIN, CREATES SKIN TONE AND PROVIDES A WATERPROOF BARRIER

- THE DERMIS LIES BELOW THE EPIDERMIS AND CONTAINS HAIR FOLLICLES, TOUGH CONNECTIVE TISSUE, AND SWEAT PORES.

- THE HYPODERMIS IS MADE OF CONNECTIVE TISSUES AND FAT

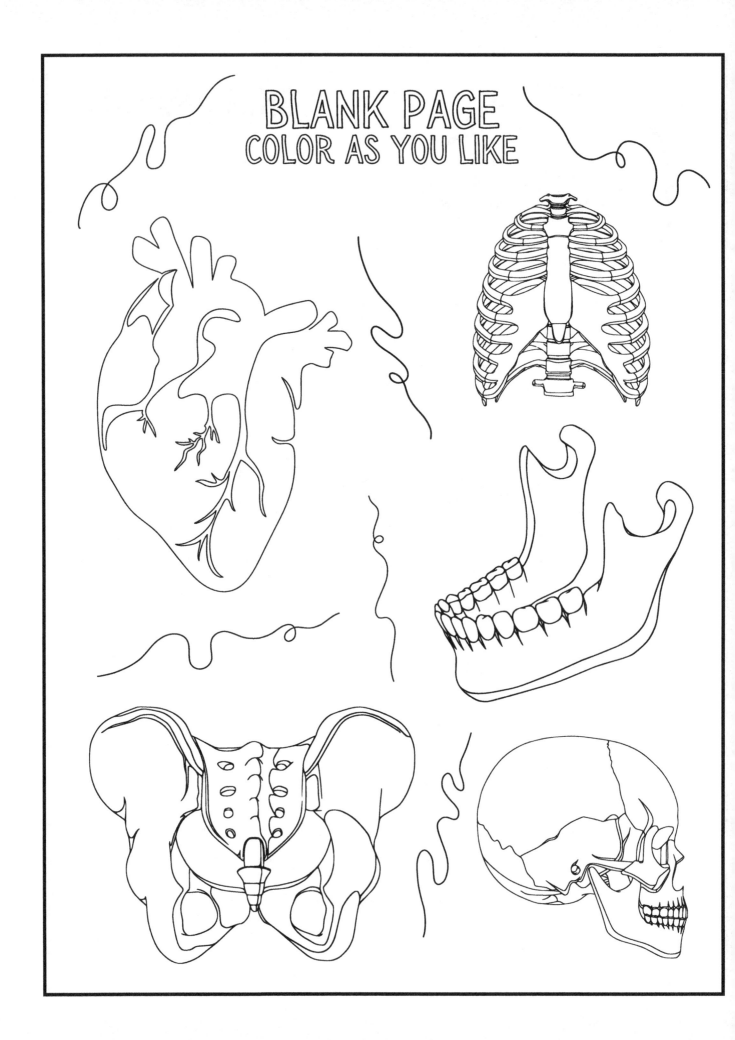

VAGUS NERVE

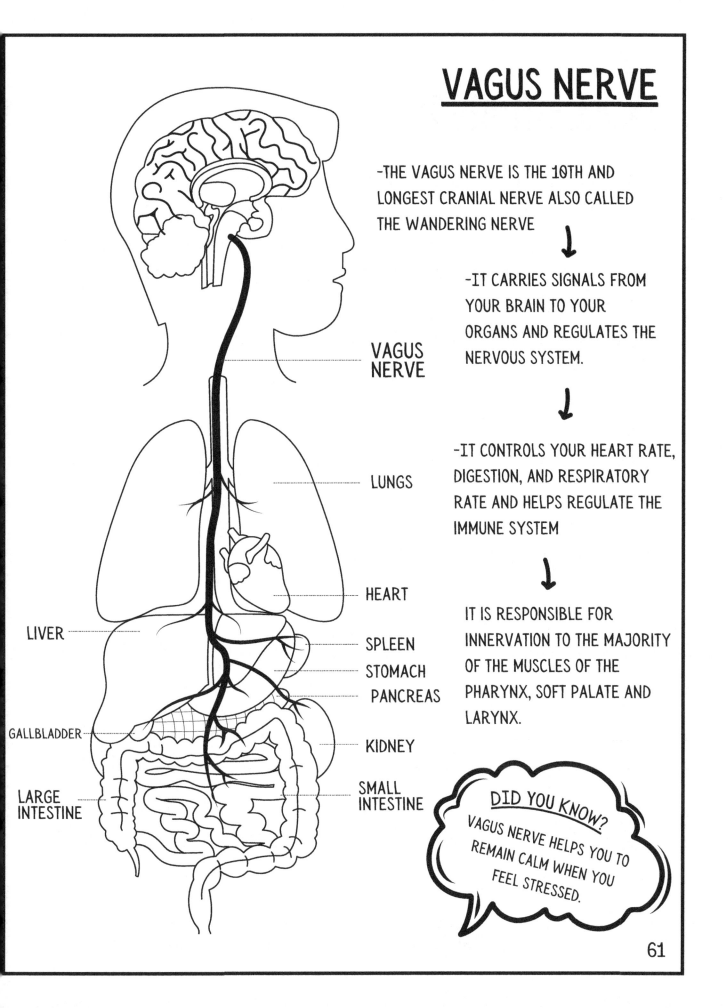

- THE VAGUS NERVE IS THE 10TH AND LONGEST CRANIAL NERVE ALSO CALLED THE WANDERING NERVE

- IT CARRIES SIGNALS FROM YOUR BRAIN TO YOUR ORGANS AND REGULATES THE NERVOUS SYSTEM.

- IT CONTROLS YOUR HEART RATE, DIGESTION, AND RESPIRATORY RATE AND HELPS REGULATE THE IMMUNE SYSTEM

IT IS RESPONSIBLE FOR INNERVATION TO THE MAJORITY OF THE MUSCLES OF THE PHARYNX, SOFT PALATE AND LARYNX.

DID YOU KNOW? VAGUS NERVE HELPS YOU TO REMAIN CALM WHEN YOU FEEL STRESSED.

FROM AUTHORS:

UNFORTUNATELY, OUR ANATOMICAL ADVENTURE IS COMING TO AN END.
SO RARELY DO WE THINK ABOUT HOW COMPLICATED AND COMPLEX OUR BODY IS.
WE HOPE THAT THIS BOOK WAS ABLE TO HELP YOU TO UNDERSTAND THE HUMAN ANATOMY, BUT MOST OF ALL, IT PROVIDED YOU WITH TIME WELL SPENT COLORING AND DEEPENING YOUR KNOWLEDGE.
FOR NOW WE HAVE TO SAY GOODBYE BUT WE HOPE TO SEE YOU AGAIN VERY VERY SOON :)

© All rights reserved to Anatomy by Heart

Made in the USA
Monee, IL
08 September 2023